ON THE WILDERNESS BATTLEFIELD
President Harding, Gen. Smedley D. Butler and John T. Goolrick

HISTORIC FREDERICKSBURG
V I R G I N I A

The Story of an Old Town

John T. Goolrick
Author of:
"The Life of General Hugh Mercer"
"Irishmen in the Civil War"
Etc.

HERITAGE BOOKS
2012

HERITAGE BOOKS
AN IMPRINT OF HERITAGE BOOKS, INC.

Books, CDs, and more—Worldwide

For our listing of thousands of titles see our website
at
www.HeritageBooks.com

A Facsimile Reprint
Published 2012 by
HERITAGE BOOKS, INC.
Publishing Division
100 Railroad Ave. #104
Westminster, Maryland 21157

Copyright © 1997 Heritage Books, Inc.

Copyright © 1922 John T. Goolrick

Originally printed by:
Whittet & Shepperson, Richmond, Virginia
Photographs by
Davis Gallery, Fredericksburg, Virginia

— Publisher's Notice —
In reprints such as this, it is often not possible to remove blemishes from the original. We feel the contents of this book warrant its reissue despite these blemishes and hope you will agree and read it with pleasure.

International Standard Book Numbers
Paperbound: 978-0-7884-0761-1
Clothbound: 978-0-7884-8982-2

This Book is Dedicated

To one who has not failed her friends, or her duty.
Who has given freely of her best.
Whose faith has not faltered, nor courage dimmed.
Who has held high her ideals; who has lighted
a pathway for those she loves.

To My Wife

FREDERICKSBURG

A Preface

FREDERICKSBURG SPRAWLS at the foot of the hills where the scented summer winds sweep over it out of the valley of brawling waters above. The grass grows lush in the meadows and tangles in the hills that almost surround it. In spring the flowers streak the lowlands, climb on the slopes, and along the ridges; and Autumn makes fair colors in the trees, shading them in blood crimson, weathered bronze, and the yellow of sunsets.

Over its shadowed streets hangs the haze of history. It is not rich nor proud, because it has not sought; it is quiet and content, because it has sacrificed. It gave its energy to the Revolution. It gave its heart to the Confederacy; and, once when it was thundered at by guns, and red flames twisted in its crumbling homes, it gave its soul and all it possessed to the South. It never abated its loyalty nor cried out its sorrows.

In Fredericksburg, and on the battlefields near it, almost thirty thousand men lay on the last couch in the shadowy forests and—we think—heard Her voice calling and comforting them. To the wounded, the Old Town gave its best, not visioning the color of their uniforms, nursing them back to life: And, broken and twisted and in poverty, it began to rebuild itself and gather up the shattered ideals of its dead past.

Out of its heart has grown simple kindness; out of its soul simple faith.

As I look out over the streets, (I knew them well when Lee and Jackson and Stuart, Lincoln and Grant and Hancock knew them too), they shimmer in the Autumn sun. Over them, as has ever seemed to me, hangs an old and haunting beauty. There may not be as great men here as long ago, but here are their descendants and the descendants of others like them. And he who comes among them will find loyal hearts and warm hand-clasps.

Ah, I know the old town. My bare feet ran along its unpaved walks and passed the cabins many a time in slavery days. I knew it in the Civil War and reconstruction days, and on and on till now: And it has not failed its duty.

Fredericksburg's history brims with achievement and adventure. It has not been tried in this volume to tell all of these. I have tried to tell a simple story, with the flame of achievement burning on the shrines and the echoes of old days sweeping through it, like low winds in the pine woods; to make men and women more vivid than dates and numbers. I have tried to be accurate and complete and to vision the past, but above all, I have loved the things of which I have written.

There is no possibility of expressing the gratitude the author feels for the aid given him by others, but he must say, briefly, that without the assistance of Miss Dora Jett, Mrs. Franklin Stearns, Mrs. John T. Goolrick, and Dr. J. N. Barney, Mr. Chester B. Goolrick and Mr. John T. Goolrick, Jr., and Mrs. Bessie Forbes Robinson, the book could not have been made as readable as we hope the public will find it. We owe just as deep thanks to Miss Sally Gravatt of the Wallace Library.

JNO. T. GOOLRICK.

Fredericksburg, Va.,
October 25, 1921.

INTRODUCTION

Rev. Robert Campbell Gilmore.

As a public speaker of wide reputation, especially on Southern themes, Hon. John T. Goolrick, Judge of the Corporation Court of Fredericksburg, Va., needs no introduction. It is my privilege to introduce him as a writer of history to an ever widening circle of readers. Other men can gather facts and put them in logical order, but few can give the history of the old town of Fredericksburg such filial sympathy and interest, such beauty of local color, as can this loyal son.

The father, Peter Goolrick, a man of fine education, came from Ireland and made his home in Fredericksburg, and was mayor of the town.

The son has always lived here. The war between the States came in his boyhood. His first connection with the Confederacy was as a messenger at the Medical Department headquarters of General Lee. Growing old enough and tiring of protected service he enlisted in Braxton's Battery of Fredericksburg Artillery. He was wounded at Fort Harrison, but recovering, returned to his command and served to the end of the war as "a distinguished private soldier," and surrendered with "The last eight thousand' at Appomattox. Since the war he has been prominently connected with Confederate affairs. At one time he was Commander of the local Camp of Veterans and is now on the staff of the Commander of all the Veterans of the South and Virginia.

After the war young Goolrick studied law, was elected Judge of the Corporation Court of Fredericksburg, and of the County Court of Spotsylvania, served for a time as Commonwealth's Attorney of Fredericksburg, and later was re-elected

Judge of the Corporation Court, which position he has held for sixteen years, and which he now holds. He has been the inceptor often, and always a worker, in every public event in the town.

This is not Judge Goolrick's first appearance as a writer. He has contributed many articles to newspapers, and magazines, and has published several books. He is thus particularly fitted to write the history of his own beloved town.

Contents

IN THE OLDER DAYS.................................	13
One by one the little cabins are built along the river bank	
AFTER THE REVOLUTION	26
In the days of its glory, the Old Town was famed and prosperous	
WAR'S WORST HORRORS	37
Shelled by 181 guns for hours, the town becomes a crumbled ruin	
THE FIRST BATTLE	48
When, at Marye's Heights and Hamilton's Crossing, war claimed her sacrifice	
AT CHANCELLORSVILLE	55
The Struggle in the Pine Woods when death struck at Southern hearts	
TWO GREAT BATTLES	64
The fearful fire swept Wilderness, and the Bloody Angle at Spottsylvania	
HEROES OF EARLY DAYS	70
The Old Town gives the first Commander, first Admiral and Great Citizens	
MEN OF MODERN TIMES	98
Soldiers, Adventurers and Sailors, Heroes and Artists, mingle here	
UNFORGOTTEN WOMEN	123
Some of Many Who Left a Record of Brilliancy, Service or Sacrifice	
AT THE RISING SUN	133
Where Famous Men Met; and Mine Host Brewed Punch and Sedition	
LAFAYETTE COMES BACK	139
After Forty Years of Failure, He Hears the Echo of His Youthful Triumph	
OLD COURT RECORD	142
Staid Documents, Writ by Hands That Are Still, Are History For Us	
ECHOES OF THE PAST	151
"Ghosts of Dead Hours, and Days That Once Were Fair"	
WHERE BEAUTY BLENDS	165
Old Gardens, at Old Mansions, Where Bloom Flowers from Long Ago	
CHURCH AND SCHOOL	173
How They Grew in the New World; Pathways to the Light	
THE CHURCH OF ENGLAND	181
First in Virginia, the Church of England Has the Longest History	
THE 250TH BIRTHDAY	188
Fredericksburg Celebrates an Anniversary	
APPENDIX	199

HISTORIC FREDERICKSBURG

In the Older Days
<small>One by one the little cabins are built along the river bank—</small>

ENVELOPED in the perfume of old English boxwood and the fragrance of still older poplars, and permeated with the charm of a two hundred and fifty year old atmosphere, the town of Fredericksburg, Virginia, nestles in the soft foliage along the banks of the Rappahannock, at the point where the turbulent waters of the upper river rush abruptly against the back-wash of the sea, an odd but pleasing mixture of the old and the new.

Subtly rich with the elegance of the past, it looks proudly back across its two and a half centuries, but it has not forgotten how to live in the present, and combines delightfully all that it has of the old with much that is new and modern.

Perhaps no other community in the country has had a more intimate and constant association with the political and historic growth of America than Fredericksburg. From the earliest Colonial period, when it was a place of importance, it traces its influence on the nation's development down through the Revolutionary war, the War of 1812, the Mexican and Civil wars and the periods of national progress between those conflicts, and even today, when the old town has lost its touch with affairs as an important community, it still can claim a close connection with events through the influence of its descendants — sons and daughters — who have gone forth in the world and achieved leadership in movements of the day that are aiding in shaping the destiny of mankind; and of these another chapter tells.

The Spanish Missionaries

But while proud of the accomplishments of these, the old town does not depend upon them for distinction. It bases its claim to this on the events with which it actually has been associated, and the importance of the part it has played in the past is proved by data found in the recorded annals of the country.

It might, indeed, if it sought historical recognition on accepted legend rather than known fact, assert an origin that antidates that of the first English permanent colony in America. A historian, writing in the Magazine of American History, says the spot now occupied by Fredericksburg was first discovered in 1571 by Spanish Missionaries, who erected there the first Christian shrine in America. It is almost certain the town was settled in 1621, three hundred years ago, but this cannot be definitely proven, and the town has not claimed it as a date in its established history. It does not claim to have had a beginning with the recorded arrival of Captain John Smith, one year after the settlement of Jamestown, but takes as its birthdate May 2d, 1671, at which time the site was legally recognized by a grant from Sir William Berkley, then Colonial governor, to John Royston and Thomas Buckner, who are looked upon as the real founders of community life at the spot now occupied by Fredericksburg.

Whether or not white men first reached the location as early as the suggested arrival of the Spanish Missionaries probably must always remain a mystery, though there are reasons to believe that this is entirely probable, as it is known that Spaniards made an early effort at colonization in Virginia, and in 1526 came up the James River from Haiti with six hundred people, and, with many negro slaves as workmen, founded the town of Miguel, near where Jamestown afterwards was establishd by Captain John Smith. It is probable that these pioneers ventured into the surrounding country, and not at all unlikely that some of them strayed as far as the falls of the Rappahannock.

But if the data are not sufficient to actually prove this early visit to the site, it is a fact of record in the diary of "Chirur-

FREDERICKSBURG FROM STAFFORD

Showing the Steeple that was Used as a Signal Station by Both Armies

geon" Bagnall, a member of the party, that Captain Smith reached the spot in 1608, one year after the establishment of Jamestown, and after successfully disputing possession of the land with a tribe of Indians, disembarked and planted a cross, later prospecting for gold and other precious metals. The diary of Smith's companions, still in existence, tells of the trip in accurate detail and from it is proven that even if the Spanish missionaries did not come as far as claimed for them, at least the Indians had recognized the natural advantages of the place by the establishment there of towns, which might have been in existence for hundreds of years.

Captain Smith made two attempts to explore the Rappahannock. The first, in June, 1608, ended when the hardy adventurer in plunging his sword into "a singular fish, like a thornback with a long tail, and from it a poison sting," ran afoul of the water monster and because of his sufferings was obliged to turn back. The second trip was started on July 24th, 1608, and was continued until the falls were reached.

Dr. Bagnall says in his diary that when near the mouth of the river, the party encountered "our old friend, Mosco, a lusty savage of Wighconscio, upon the Patawomeck," who accompanied them as guide and interpreter, and upon reaching the falls did splendid service against the unfriendly Indians, "making them pause upon the matter, thinking by his bruit and skipping there were many savages." In the fighting Captain Smith's party captured a wounded Indian and much to the disgust of the cheerful Mosco, who wished to dispatch him forthwith, spared his life and bound his wounds. This work of mercy resulted in a truce with the Redmen, which made possible the final undisturbed settlement of the land by the whites, the prisoner interceding for Smith and his party.

Captain Smith's first landing on the upper river probably was directly opposite what now is the heart of Fredericksburg. Dr. Bagnall's diary says:

"Between Secobeck and Massawteck is a small isle or two, which causes the river to be broader than ordinary; there it

About The Indian Villages

pleased God to take one of our company, called Master Featherstone, that all the time he had been in this country had behaved himself honestly, valiently and industriously, where in a little bay, called Featherstone's bay, we buried him with a volley of shot * * *·

"The next day we sailed so high as our boat would float, there setting up crosses and graving our names on trees."

Captain Quinn, in his excellent History of Fredericksburg, says that Featherstone's bay "is in Stafford, opposite the upper end of Hunter's island," but it is probable he did not closely examine facts before making this statement, as his own location of other places mentioned in Dr. Bagnall's diary serves to disprove his contention as to the whereabouts of the bay.

"Seacobeck," Captain Quinn says, "was just west of the city almshouse." The almshouse was then situated where the residence of the President of the State Normal School now stands. Massawteck, Captain Quinn locates as "just back of Chatham." If his location of these two places is correct, it is clear that the "small isle or two," which the diary says was located between them, must have been at a point where a line drawn from the President's residence, at the Normal School, to "just back of Chatham" would intersect the river, which would be just a little above the present location of Scott's island, and that Featherstone's bay occupied what now are the Stafford flats, extending along the river bank from nearly opposite the silk mill to the high bank just above the railroad bridge and followed the course of Claibourne's Run inland, to where the land again rises. The contours of the land, if followed, here show a natural depression that might easily have accommodated a body of water, forming a bay.

There are other evidences to bear out this conclusion. Dr. Bagnall's diary says: "The next day we sailed so high as our boat would float." It would have been an impossibility to proceed "high" (meaning up) the river from Hunter's island in boats, even had it been possible to go as high as that point.

Establishment of the Town

Notwithstanding contradictory legend, the falls of the Rappahannock have been where they are today for from five to one hundred thousand years, and there is no evidence whatever to indicate that Hunter's Island ever extended into tidewater, the formation of the banks of the river about that point giving almost absolute proof that it did not.

No authentic data can be found to prove the continued use of the site as a settlement from Smith's visit forward, though the gravestone of a Dr. Edmond Hedler, bearing the date 1617, which was found near Potomac run in Stafford county, a few miles from the town, would indicate that there were white settlers in the section early in the 17th century, and if this is true there is every reason to believe the falls of the Rappahannock were not without their share, as the natural advantages of the place for community settlement would have been appealing and attractive to the colonists, who would have been quick to recognize them.

In 1622, according to Howe's history, Captain Smith proposed to the London Company to provide measures "to protect all their planters from the James to the Potowmac rivers." a territory that included the Rappahannock section, which can be taken as another indication of the presence of settlers in the latter.

The first legal record of the place as a community is had in 1671 — strangely enough just one hundred years after the reported coming of the Spaniards — when Thomas Royston and John Buckner were granted, from Sir William Berkley, a certain tract of land at "the falls of the Rappahannock." This was on May 2d, and shortly afterward, together with forty colonists, they were established on what is now the heart of Fredericksburg, but known in those remote times as "Leaseland." This is the date that Fredericksburg officially takes as its birthday, though additional evidence that colonists already were in that vicinity is had in the fact that the boundaries of the land described in the grant from Governor Berkley to the two early settlers, ended where the lands of one Captain Lawrence Smith began.

Major Lawrence Smith's Fort

Three or four years after the grant was made to Buckner and Royston the "Grande Assemblie at James Cittie" took official cognizance of the Colony by ordering Major Lawrence Smith and one hundred and eleven men to the Falls of the Rappahannock for the purpose of protecting the colonists. Records in regard to this say, "At a Grande Assemblie at James Cittie, between the 20th of September, 1674, and the 17th of March, 1675, it was ordered that one hundred and eleven men out of Gloucester be garrisoned at one ffort or place of defense, at or near the falls of the Rappahannock river, of which ffort Major Lawrence Smith is to be captain or chief commander." It was also ordered that "the ffort be furnished with four hundred and eight pounds of powder and fourteen hundred pounds of shott."

A few years later, in 1679, Major Smith was authorized by the Jamestown government to mark out, below the falls of the Rappahannock, a strip of land one mile long and one-fourth of a mile wide, to be used as a colony and, together with eight commissioners, he was empowered to hold court and administer justice. Within this confine he was instructed to build habitations for two hundred and fifty men, fifty of whom were to be kept well armed and ready to respond to the tap of a drum. It would appear that the "ffort" mentioned in the earlier meeting of the "Grande Assemblie" was not built until this year. The contention that it was erected on the Stafford side of the river seems to be without any foundation of fact.

That the community was now growing seems to be proven by the fact that the same act, defining the limits mentioned above, also mentioned a larger district, defined as extending three miles above the fort and two miles below it for a distance of four miles back, over which Major Smith and his commissioners were to have jurisdiction. Two years later, in 1681, the little town received a great impetus when two hundred families came to join the colony. From this time forward, the community began to take an important part in the life of the Colonies.

Falmouth's Fast Growth

In 1710, upon the invitation of Baron de Graffenried, a friend of Governor Spotswood, twelve German families came to America and settled on the Rapidan river, eighteen miles above Fredericksburg, opening the first iron mines and establishing the first iron works in America. They named the place Germanna, and, according to an account left by one of the party, "packed all their provisions from Fredericksburg," then the principal trading point of the section.

In 1715, Governor Spotswood and the now-famed "Knights of the Golden Horseshoe," started from Germanna (some of them came through Fredericksburg en route and stopped with Austin Smith). Assembling at Germanna they left on September 24th and continued across the Blue Ridge mountains to the Valley of Virginia. An interesting account of the trip, which has been made the theme of song and story, and even the basis of a secret society, can be found in the diary of John Fountaine, a member of the party.

For a period nothing seems to have happened to the community of sufficient importance to be recorded, and for the next few years the imagination must supply the story of the settlement. It probably was a village of irregular, straggling streets and indifferent houses, with a population that struggled for a living by trading, trapping and other pursuits of that day. Its stores were likely very good for those times, but across the river it had a rival in its neighbor, Falmouth, which as a place of importance was fast catching up with it, and soon was destined to pass it, for in 1720, seven years earlier than "The Leaseland," it received its charter from the House of Burgesses at Williamsburg, who vested its government in seven trustees.

If not as a political and social center, at least as a trading point, Falmouth had soon superceded Fredericksburg. It was the market for all the grain of the upper country, which by this time was beginning to be settled, and was in direct commercial communication with England, Europe and the West Indies by ocean-going vessels, which, when under 140 tons

"Leaseland" Is Chartered

burden, could come up to its wharves. It was a great milling center and its merchants began to grow prosperous and wealthy, one of them, Mr. Bazil Gordon, accumulating the first million dollars ever made in America, though he was the product of a little later date than that now under consideration.

Grain brought out of Falmouth in boats larger than 140 tons was first put upon barges or flat boats of large capacity, which were conveyed down the river to waiting vessels and transferred by slave labor. The stories heard of large vessels docking at the Falmouth wharves are apocryphal; no boat of great tonnage ever got as far as Falmouth. This may account for Fredericksburg's final supremacy over Falmouth, which doubtless came about the time the first ferry was started, permitting the planters to cross the river with their grain and load directly to the waiting vessels, thus saving time and work, valuable considerations even in those days of abundant leisure and cheap slave labor.

But, while Falmouth was progressing "Leaseland" was also making strides, and in 1727 it became of sufficient importance to receive its charter from the House of Burgesses, and was named in honor of Frederick, Prince of Wales, son of George II. The Prince died before ascending the throne, but his son became George III., and it was thus from the domination of the son of the Prince for whom their town was named that the patriotic people of the little village later plotted to free themselves. The act giving the town a charter names John Robinson, Henry Willis, Augustine Smith, John Taliaferro, Henry Beverly, John Waller and Jeremiah Crowder as trustees, and the streets were named for members of the Royal family, names which fortunately endure today, despite an attempt made some years ago to modernize the town and discard the beautiful and significant old names in favor of the less distinguished and uglier method of numerical and alphabetical designations.

Settlers now were rapidly coming into the community which was growing in importance. In 1732, Colonel Byrd

FROM MRS. WASHINGTON'S FARM

One Sees, Across the River, the Homes of Such Families as the Mercer's, Weedon's, Mortimer's

"Town Fairs" Are Begun

owner of vast tracts where now stands the magnificent city of Richmond, an important man in the Colonial life of Virginia, came to Fredericksburg, calling on his friend, Colonel Henry Willis, "top man of the town," as Colonel Byrd refers to him in his very interesting account of the visit preserved to posterity. Colonel Byrd was impressed by Fredericksburg, particularly by the stone jail, which, he said, seemed strong enough "to hold Jack Shepherd" and with the versatility of one Sukey Livingstone, or Levinston, doctress and coffee woman. Some believe that the old stone building at the Free Bridge head is the jail referred to.

The seat of justice which had been located at Germanna, was this year moved to Fredericksburg, St. George's parish established and the church erected, with Rev. Patrick Henry, uncle of the famous orator, as its first rector.

In 1738 the House of Burgesses authorized the holding twice annually of town fairs for the sale of cattle, provisions, goods, wares and all kinds of merchandise, and it is easy to understand how these affairs became the most important events in the life of the village, attracting plantation owners from miles and taking on a social as well as business aspect. And as the act also provided that all persons attending these fairs should be immune from arrest for two days previous and two days subsequent to the events, except for capital offenses or breaches of the peace, suits, controversies and quarrels that might arise during the events, it can well be imagined that they were lively and exciting gatherings.

One year later the trustees found it necessary to purchase additional land for the accommodation of the growing population but a bargain was struck with Henry Willis, "the top man of the town," and John Lewis only after the House of Burgesses had taken up the matter deciding the ownership of the lands in question and fixing the sum to be paid Willis at fifteen pounds and Lewis at five pounds, not a bad total price, considering the survey shows that only three acres were bought.

Masonry Is Established

The town had now grown to such importance as a trading point that the establishment of direct connections with the Stafford shore was made necessary, and in 1748 the first ferry was authorized by law. Evidently from this time forward the town began to forge ahead of its thriving neighbor, Falmouth, for the lessened expense of transferring grain directly to the waiting ships made it more attractive as a market and many of the up-country people who formerly had sold their gain and traded in Falmouth, now crossed on the ferry and spent their money with the merchants of Fredericksburg. The establishment of Masonry in 1752, at which time the lodge was known as "The Lodge of Fredericksburg," points to the growing importance of the place; and that the Colonial citizens were keenly alive to the benefits to be derived from attracting industry to their towns is attested to by an act of the General Assembly, passed in 1759, to encourage the arts and manufactury in the Colonies, which set up a premium of five hundred pounds to be awarded the citizen making the best ten hogsheads of wine in any one year, within eight years from the passage of the act. A number of citizens of the town contributed to the fund, among them George Washington, who gave two pounds.

In the Indian wars of 1755-57, Fredericksburg became an important depot and rendezvous for troops. Recruits, provisions, supplies and ordnances were sent to the town in quantities, and on April 15th, 1757, Governor Dinwiddie ordered Colonel George Washington to send two hundred men there to be "Thence sent by vessels to South Carolina, to treat with curtesy the Indians at Fort London, and to send them out in scalping parties with such number of men as you can spare."

But now the peaceable growth and prosperity of the village were to be halted. Dissatisfaction with the government in England began to grow, and there were murmurings of discontent and resentment, not by any means indulged in by all the citizens, for large numbers were still utterly loyal to the Crown, and those who opposed its policies congregated to themselves, meeting in secret or standing in little groups about the streets to give vent to their feelings.

The Revolution Gathers

One well-known place for the meeting of "Revolutionists" was the Rising Sun tavern still standing in good order, at that time kept by "Mine Host," George Weedon. This famed old Tavern is told of in another chapter. It is almost certain that at this tavern the rough draft was made of a resolution to be later passed in a public town meeting, which was tantamount to a declaration of independence, and which was passed twenty-one days before the famous Mecklenburg declaration and more than a year before that of the American congress.

These resolutions were adopted on the 29th day of April, 1775, amidst the greatest public excitement. News of the battle of Lexington, fought on the 20th of April, and of the removal by Lord Dunmore of twenty barrels of powder from the public magazine at Williamsburg to the English frigate "Fowey," then lying near Yorktown, which occurred one day after the battle of Lexington, had just reached Fredericksburg. Immediately the citizens showed their indignation. More than six hundred men from the town and the surrounding country armed themselves and sent a courier to General Washington, then at Williamsburg, offering their services in defense of the Colonies. Delegates were also dispatched to Richmond to ascertain the true state of affairs, and to find out at what point the men should report. The men stayed under arms and in readiness to move at short notice until General Washington transmitted a message, advising that they restrain from any hostilities until a congress could be called to decide upon a general plan of defense. This advice was received by a council of more than a hundred men, representing fourteen companies (the number under arms having by this time grown), which decided by a majority of one to disperse for the present, but to keep themselves in readiness for a call. Many of them afterwards joined the armies of General Washington.

Material preparations for the conflict that everyone, even the Tories, now felt was certain, were made by the establishment at the town of the first small arms manufactury in America, which was located on what now is known as Gunnery Green. Colonel Fielding Lewis, brother-in-law of Gen-

"The Gunnery" Is Built

eral Washington, was one of the commissioners in charge of the gunnery and active in its management.

With the coming of the Gunnery, and the formation of companies of troops, the peaceful atmosphere of Fredericksburg quickly changed to one of a militaristic aspect. Recruits drilled in the street, the manufacture of arms was rushed, supplies were received and stored, couriers, with news from other parts of the country, dashed in to acquaint the eager townspeople with events, and those loyal to the Colonies went bravely about with every kind of war preparation, while those inclined to Toryism kept quiet and to themselves, or moved away with their families, hoping, and probably succeeding in many cases, in reaching England before the whole country was affected by the war, in which the part played by Fredericksburg and its citizens was of the utmost importance. The town gave to the Revolution an unusually large proportion of troops and many of the great leaders.

During the Revolution, although Fredericksburg men were the leaders of the Army, no fighting occurred here and the period was not one of danger for the town, but was one of anxiety for the inhabitants. Tarleton passed close to this city on his raid towards Charlottesville, and Lafayette and his men built the road still known as "The Marquis Road," through the Wilderness toward Orange.

Recently three soldiers, whose uniform buttons testify they were Hessians, were dug up near Spotsylvania Court House. A prison camp existed about two miles from here on the Plank Road from which Washington recruited some artisans to do the interior decorating in the home of his beloved sister, Betty, at Kenmore.

Several Regiments went from Fredericksburg. General William Woodford (see sketch of life) was elected Commander of the first. Among his descendants are the late Marion Willis, Mayor Willis and Mr. Benj. Willis. General Hugh Mercer was chosen Commander of the third regiment, and James Monroe, of Fredericksburg (afterwards president) was Lieut.-Colonel, while Thomas Marshall, father of Chief Justice Marshall, was Major. The other Virginia Regiment was not recruited here. It was commanded by Patrick Henry.

Although it furnished two of the first three Virginia Regiments, and half of America's Generals, as well as the Commanding General, Fredericksburg was not a war center. Its history during that period will be found in the lives of the men it produced, elsewhere in this book.

It did give most material aid by furnishing arms from the "Gunnery" of Col. Fielding Lewis, and was generous in its financial aid, and always ready for attack.

After the Revolution

In the days of its glory, the Old Town was famed and prosperous

The first mention of Fredericksburg in the annals of the new Republic is an act of the legislature in 1781, incorporating the town and vesting the powers of its government in the hands of a mayor and commonality, consisting of a council and board of aldermen. Courts were established and provision made for future elections of its officials.

The first mayor was Charles Mortimer, and the Board of Aldermen consisted of William Williams, John Sommerville, Charles Dick, Samuel Roddy and John Julien, who, together with the mayor, were also justices of the peace, and required to hold a hustings court monthly. John Legg was appointed sergeant of the court and corporation, and John Richards and James Jarvis constables. The town's initial commonwealth's attorney, John Minor, is said to have been the first man to offer in any legislative body of the country a bill for the emancipation of the slaves.

The first action of the court is interesting, especially in these times. It was giving license to five persons to conduct taverns, immediately followed by an act to regulate them by establishing prices for alcoholic, vinous and fermented beverages. There is no mention of opening or closing hours, Sunday selling, selling to minors or any of the later and stricter regulations, and the prices to be charged are in terms of pounds, or parts, per gallon. The American bar was unknown then and probably even in the taverns and tap rooms, little liquor was sold by the drink. Some of the prices established translated into dollars, were West Indian rum, per gallon, $3.34; brandy, $1.67; good whiskey, $1.00; good beer, $0.67 and so on.

The Famed "Peace Ball"

Having taken care that the tavern keepers could not charge too much for drink, the court now provided that they should not over charge for food served, placing the score for a "single diet" at twenty-five cents, a most reasonable sum according to modern standards.

While having the power to regulate, the court was not without regulation from a superior source as the articles of incorporation show that in case of misconduct on the part of the mayor or any member of the board, the others would have power to remove him after the charges had been fully proved, and it further stipulated that should any person elected to office fail or refuse to serve, he should be fined according to the following scale: mayor, fifty pounds; recorder, forty pounds; alderman, thirty pounds; councilman, twenty-five pounds. In 1782 an amendment was passed by the legislature, enlarging the jurisdiction of the court to include all territory within one mile of the town limits.

Fredericksburg was not long in recovering from the effects of the Revolution. It had suffered no physical damage, though it had lost a great deal of actual and potential value in the deaths of citizens who gave their lives for the cause. A magnificent Peace Ball was held, in 1784, in the assembly room over the old City Hall, at Main Street and "Market Alley," which was attended by General Washington, General Lafayette, Rochambeau, Washington's mother, who came leaning on his arm and all the notables and fashionables of the country. The town was soon again a thriving hustling center of trade and business.

New enterprises came as requirements of the times made themselves felt. In 1786 the Virginia Herald made its appearance, the first newspaper published in the town, and about the same time whipping posts, ducking stools, and pillories were established to keep down the criminal tendencies of the unlawfully inclined. In 1789 an act was passed, empowering the trustees of the Fredericksburg Academy to raise by lottery $4,000 to defray the expenses of erecting a building on the

Commercial Development

grounds for the accommodation of professors, a method of raising money that modern morals has outlawed. In 1795 the Episcopal Charity School was established by Archibald McPherson one of the splendid men of the town and in 1799 the town experienced its first serious fire, which was held by some to have been the work of an incendiary and by others as due to a wooden chimney. The council in an effort to assuredly exclude all danger of another such from either source, offered a reward of $500. for conviction of the incendiary, and passed an ordinance abolishing wooden chimneys, and stove pipes sticking through windows or the sides of houses, provided the buildings were not fire proof.

From 1800 to 1850 Fredericksburg was the principal depot of trade and commerce for all that region between the Rappahannock river and the counties of Orange, Culpeper, Rapidan, Madison and Fauquier in addition to the contiguous territory and the great section lying between the town and the Chesapeake bay. Commerce with the upper country, however, was the most productive, for the lower country people were in close connection with the rivers and, as in those days all shipping was done by water ways, they shipped from wharves along the Rappahannock near their homes. They received much of their goods in this manner and were not so dependent upon the town as the upper country people who were forced to bring their products to Fredericksburg by wagon trains, which lumbered slowly down with their burdens of grain, produce and tobacco, and having unloaded and tarried awhile, lumbered back even more slowly, loaded with groceries, wines, liquors, household stores, plantation supplies, dry goods and merchandise for the country stores.

These wagons were of huge dimensions, "their curving bodies being before and behind at least twelve feet from the ground" according to one writer. They had canvas covers and were drawn by four horses always, sometimes six and eight, carrying jangling bells upon their collars. As many as two hundred of them were often on the streets or in the

Fires Sweep the Town

wagon yards of Fredericksburg at one time, making prosperity for the energetic merchants of that distant day, and bringing business for the many vessels, some of them large three masted schooners, which came from all parts of the globe to anchor at the wharves.

At about this time Fredericksburg received two serious blows that greatly retarded its progress and prosperity. The first was in 1808, when nearly half the town was destroyed by a fire which broke out at the corner of Princess Anne and Lewis streets, where the Shepherd residence now stands, and fanned by a high wind quickly roared its way through the inflammable houses, such as most of the residences then were, until the town was half in ashes. At the outbreak of the fire most of the citizens were attending the races at "Willis Field," just below the town, and before they could get back it had gained such headway that their efforts to check it were ineffectual. It is said the fire was caused by the overturning of a candle in the kitchen of the Stannard home, occupying the present site of the Shepherd residence, where refreshments were being prepared for the funeral of Mr. Stannard, and that the remains were gotten out of the house only with great difficulty on the part of the mourners. In those days funerals were accompanied by feasts, at which cake in sombre wrappings and wine in glasses with long black ribbons tied to the stems, were served.

Much of the brick construction on the upper business section of Main street, and a number of residences known as Colonial, are results of that fire, but deserve to be called Colonial as that period, architectually speaking, extended until about the year 1812. The Shepherd residence, of course, was built following the fire; the old Doswell home, now occupied by Mr. A. W. Rowe, probably was erected afterwards and the old Marye home, now owned by Mr. A. L. Jenkins, has a corner stone bearing the date 1812, the residence formerly occupying that site having been burned. However, most of the older residences in Fredericksburg antedate the fire, and are of an earlier Colonial period.

During The War of 1812

Another blow was the War of 1812, and though, as in the case of the Revolution, the city did not suffer actual physical damage, its business and trade were interrupted and severely decreased, if not totally stopped, due to the English dominance of the seas and during the course of that conflict, the commercial life must have been slow and stagnant.

Fredericksburg itself was for a time threatened when the English admiral, Cockburn, made a raid up the Rappahannock. Many thought his objective was Fredericksburg and General William Madison, brother of the President, summoned a small force which took up positions of defense, from which to repel the raider, but he never got up the river as far as the city, turning when much lower down and putting back to sea for a cause which history has not assigned. During this war, as had been the case in the Revolution, and was to be in the Civil war to come, the Mercer home, now occupied by Councilman George W. Heflin, which stands on an eminence on lower Main street commanding a splendid view of the river, was used as a post from which to watch for the approach of enemy ships, a use that has given it the name of "The Sentry Box."

Following the War of 1812, Fredericksburg's trade revived and increased, and the city settled down to a full enjoyment of that remarkably cultural era — the only classical civilization America has ever known — which lasted until the Civil war and which has been made famous in song and story and the history of the old South. The families of the early settlers had by now become wealthy; the plantation masters owned hundreds of slaves, farmed thousands of acres and lived in their handsome old Colonial mansions in the most magnificent style the times could afford. Surrounded by many servants and all the comforts known to the day, they entertained lavishly, kept splendidly stocked wine cellars, boasted of private race courses and keen thoroughbred hunters and racers, and, as the business of the plantations was largely in the hands of overseers, they were gentlemen of splendid leisure with an abundance of time opportunity and means to

THE HOME OF JAMES MONROE

Who Began His Official Career as a Councilman in Fredericksburg, and Became President

devote to sports, politics and literature. Most of them were educated abroad and were learned in the classics, clever and entertaining conversationalists, beautiful riders, excellent shots, and when not engaged in social or literary pursuits that kept them indoors, enjoyed the sports of the field, hunting to the hounds, gunning for quail, deer, bear, wild turkey or duck, or fishing in the abundantly supplied streams tributary to the Potomac and Rappahannock rivers. Hard drinking was not unusual among them, but they were men of the highest sense of honor and principle, and were always true to an obligation.

While the townspeople did not enjoy life quite so lavishly as their plantation neighbors, they were not far behind; entertaining frequently and hospitably and mingling freely with the people from the country.

But though it was a gay and carefree day, the times were not without their troubles. In 1822 the town was again visited by fire, this time originating at the site of the present Brent's store, at Main and George streets, destroying the entire business block encompassed between Main and Princess Anne and George and Hanover streets. Recovery from this fire was rapid. The merchants were financially substantial and quickly rebuilt the burned area.

As early as 1822, Fredericksburg was an important postal point, the mail for five states being assorted and distributed in the city and sent thence to its final destination. The conduct of Postmaster General Meigs in regard to increasing the compensation of carriers on the Fredericksburg route without authorization from Congress, was the subject of an investigation by that body, but he was exonerated when it was explained that the increase was necessary because the mail had become so heavy that carriers were no longer able to handle it on horse back, being compelled to use surries, an added expense to them which justified the additional pay.

James Monroe, a former resident, lawyer and councilman of Fredericksburg, was at that time President of the United States, and though the town doubtless was a naturally

The Town Grows Richer

important postal distribution, it may have been that the President's influence had some bearing on the selection of the place which had given him his political start.

For the next decade, the trade and commercial life of the town increased. The merchants and manufacturers — by this time several large industries of this character being in operation — were busy and prosperous and had begun to grow either wealthy, measured in the standards of the time, or were in very comfortable circumstances, while the citizenry, generally, was prosperous and free from want. The town was compactly built, many of its structures now being of brick, and was regularly laid out. The public buildings consisted of a courthouse, market house, clerks office, the Episcopal Orphan Asylum, the Episcopal, Presbyterian, Methodist, Baptist and Reform Baptist Church. It had two banks, one female and one male academy of the higher class; a water system supplied through pipes from Poplar Spring. And the upper river canal was being built, a public enterprise from which great results were expected and which was to extend about forty miles up the Rappahannock. Gold was being mined in considerable quantities in upper Spotsylvania and lower Culpeper counties and brought to Fredericksburg in exchange for goods, and a generally thriving trade was being done, chiefly in grain, bacon, tobacco and other farm products for export. One writer has computed the city's annual exports at that time as averaging four million dollars, and Government statistics show that there were in the town in 1840, seventy-three stores, two tanneries, one grist mill, two printing plants, four semi-weekly newspapers, five academies with 256 students, and seven schools with 165 scholars. The population in that year was 3,974. Ten years previous it had been 3,308, divided as follows: whites, 1,797; slaves, 1,124; free blacks, 387.

From 1840 until the middle fifties, prosperity was continued. The canal was completed and had brought about an increased business at a lower cost. A railroad was in operation from Richmond through Fredericksburg to Aquia Creek, and steamboats had to some extent taken the place of sailing vessels as a means of water transportation, meaning quicker trips with greater burdens. In 1851 the legislature passed an act empowering the town to extend its limits, which was done according to a survey made by William Slaughter, and though that was more than seventy years ago, and though the population has since more than doubled, overflowing the limits and encroaching on the adjoining county, the limits have not again been enlarged.

In 1855 Fredericksburg's trade had ceased to grow at a rate equal to its average yearly increase for the previous twenty years, a condition for which the business men of that day were not altogether responsible, but which rather was brought about by the new commercial era the country and world was just entering — the era of railroad transportation, which quickly and cheaply, in comparison to past charges, carried the staples of the farm to the ports of the sea where waiting vessels stood ready to spread their sable sails on voyages to foreign markets. This era created the importance of the seaport and spelled the doom, as important shipping points, of the tidewater cities — those which had been located at the point where mountain torrent and still water meet in order to get both the advantage of power production and trade routes.

It is true that the business men of the city made the serious mistake about this period of building a plank road into one portion of the upper country from which they derived much trade, instead of building a railroad, for just a little later transportation by wagon train for export purposes had nearly entirely given away to transportation by rail, and Fredericksburg was utterly without such connection with its greatest field of trade, which soon was largely converted into other channels by the railroads now beginning to practically surround the town at a distance of approximately forty miles to the west. The single railroad passing through Fredericksburg had no coast terminal. Throughout its short length it paralleled the coast, offering no means of shipping for export, which comprised most of the business of the day. The plantation owners of the upper country who had dealt nearly entirely

The War Ends Prosperity

in Fredericksburg, now found it cheaper to haul to the railroad passing through their country and soon Fredericksburg was belted by little towns to the west. When later the P. F. & P. R. R. was built to Orange, it did not save the situation and except for lumber and ties, a trade it still largely enjoys, it has never hauled much to Fredericksburg for export, though it did help the city considerably in the matter of retail business.

Trade, however, had not ceased entirely to grow, nor the town to increase. In 1860 its population was nearly 5,000 persons, its business men still were active and prosperous and, but for the Civil war which was to come, they doubtless would have found a way out of the commercial difficulty confronting them and a different history of the town from that time forward might have been written.

But over the course of a few years preceding this date, the community was troubled and torn by political strife and moral dissention. Black and ominous on the horizon of men's thoughts loomed the slave question, perplexing the country's leaders and giving threats of the red carnage that was to follow. A carnage that cost millions in men and money, caused unreckoned anguish and suffering, and retarded the growth of the South to such an extent that at the end of the following fifty years it had only just begun to emerge from the black shadow cast over it by the war.

By the end of the fifty's, trade had almost ceased, a spirit of patriotism for the Southland superseded that of commercial enterprise, the quietness of the soft old Colonial town was broken by wild public meetings; soon the call of a bugle floated softly across the still air and the heavy monotonous tread of feet sounded against the ground in unison to the beating of drums, and though the citizens had been loyal to the Union, sending by nearly a two-thirds majority a Union man to the State convention, they made ready for the inevitable conflict, and when the flame of war burst on the country like a flaring torch, they threw in their lots with the land of their nativity and bravely shouldering their arms, marched

A Town in "No Man's Land"

away from their homes to a fate that would bring them death or sorrow, and reduce their land to a shambles. The story of the Civil war as it effected this town is told in other chapters which follow this.

For many years after the Civil war, Fredericksburg's connection with the great tragedy was told in the lines of patient suffering that webbed the faces of the older generation. It was a town of sombre, black figures — the widows and daughters of soldiers — gentle creatures who moved about in quiet dignity, bravely concealing the anguish hidden in their hearts, and smilingly making the best of such disordered conditions and distressing circumstances as before they had never known. It was a town filled with broken, crushed men, ill fitted for the harsher demands of their new lives; men once rich but now suddenly tossed from the foundations that always had sustained them, who found themselves aliens in an unknown and unfriendly world.

Blackened, scarred ruins of what once had been magnificent homes remained mute, grim evidences of the ghastly horror and the quaint old town was stunned and still, a tragic wreck of its one time beauty. But as best it could it gathered up the tangled threads of its existence and for the next decade struggled dumbly and blindly against the terrible disadvantages imposed upon it by the ruthlessness of war.

When the war came with Spain, it showed that the hurt of the Civil strife was gone, when its young men marched proudly through the streets to take their parts in the crisis; sent on their missions of patriotism with the feeble but sincere cheers of aged Confederate veterans ringing in their ears.

With the beginnings of the 20th century, Fredericksburg gave visable evidence of its recovery from the wounds of war. Its business men had accumulated sufficient capital to revive trade, at least partially, on its past scale; additional industries were started, new homes and buildings sprang up and there was the beginning of a general and steady improvement.

A Change in Government

In 1909 a group of progressive citizens, among whom one of the most earnest was the late Henry Warden, a man of immense usefulness, realized their ambition and the consummation of an aim for which they had fought for years, when the old form of councilmanic government was abolished in favor of the City Manager form, Fredericksburg being one of the first small cities in the country to adopt it. Since its inauguration, the city has prospered and improved. Well laid granolithic sidewalks are placed throughout its business and residential sections, splendid hard gravel streets, topped with smooth asphalt binding, have replaced the old mud roadways, the water system has been enlarged and improved, fire protection increased and other municipal improvements made that have taken the town out of the class of sleepy provincial hamlets and made of it a modern little city. New hotels of the finest type, business enterprises and industrial concerns have come to give it new life and color, but with all this it still retains much that is sweet and old and is filled with the charm and elegance of the past.

Though it has just celebrated its two hundred and fiftieth birthday, the anniversary of a time when America was only beginning to give promise of its brilliant future, a time when the country was young and weak, but when manhood was strong and courage held high the torch of hope, Fredericksburg looks forward to the future with eager longing, confident that in the mirror of its past is the story of the time to come.

War's Worst Horrors

Shelled by 181 guns for hours, the town becomes a crumbled ruin

Fredericksburg is the point through which the railway and the roads to Richmond pass, and is half way between Washington and the Southern city. During the Civil war the possession of the town was an advantage not to be despised, and so from the beginning the two great armies of the North and South were contenders for the town.

The first attempt toward Fredericksburg was made June 1, 1861, when Federal gunboats and a small cavalry force were defeated, in an attempt to land troops at Aquia Creek, by General Daniel Ruggles, C. S. A., in command of the Department of Fredericksburg. This was the first skirmish of the war, in Virginia, and occurred nine days before "Big Bethel" and seven weeks after Virginia seceded.

On the nineteenth of April, 1862, the Stafford hills were taken by the Federals, and on April 27th General Marsena R. Patrick marched troops into the town and placed it under military rule. General Patrick treated the citizens with consideration and under his rule there was but little complaint of oppression. He was, in fact, generally admired for his fair treatment of the populace.

But with the coming of the conceited and inhuman General Pope, who followed McClellan in command of the Federal army, all that was changed. From that time forward this quiet old city between the hills, with its splendid homes, its old silver and china and tapistry and paintings, its great trees and broad streets, was to know every cruelty, horror, and depredation of war.

General Pope, driven back by the Confederates, moved through Fauquier and Culpeper counties to Fredericksburg, and immediately upon securing the town, his subordinates scoured the city and arrested nineteen of the most prominent men, alleging no crime but stating frankly that it was done in reprisal for the arrest by the Confederates of Major Charles Williams of Fredericksburg, who was held in Richmond to prevent him from aiding the enemy. These men were sent to the old Capital Prison at Washington, where they were held from early in August to late September in 1862, and were then released in exchange for Major Williams and others. There were Rev. W. F. Broaddus,, D. D., James McGuire, Charles Welford, Thomas F. Knox, Beverly T. Gill, James H. Bradley, Thomas B. Barton, Benjamin Temple, Lewis Wrenn, Michael Ames, John Coakley, John H. Roberts, John J. Berrey, Dr. James Cooke, John F. Scott, Montgomery Slaughter, (Mayor), George H. C. Rowe, Wm. H. Norton, Abraham Cox.

Fredericksburg was evacuated in August, 1862, when the Northern soldiers were drawn up in line and marched out of town. A great burden was lifted from the community. Heavy explosions marked the blowing up of the two bridges. On September 4th, an advance guard of Confederate cavalry rode into the town amid shouts of welcome.

The relief was but for a short period. On November 10th, Captain Dalgren's (Federal) dragoons crossed the river above Falmouth and clattered down Main street and met a small force of Confederates under Col. Critcher, who drove them back. But General Burnside's whole army was following and in a few days held the Stafford hills.

Fredericksburg and the country immediately about it was fought over, marched over, shelled and ravaged and desolated. The town became a dreary military outpost of battered, falling walls and charred timbers, of soldiers, now in gray, now in blue. Under its streets and in yards hundreds of dead were buried to be now and again, in after years, unearthed. No other American city ever suffered as did this formerly prosperous town.

The situation, from a military standpoint, was this: Southeastward of the city the Rappahannock broadens, so that

THE SLAVE BLOCK
Commerce Street, Where Slaves were Sold. The "Step" is Deeply Worn By The Feet of those Who Mounted It

it is not easily bridged, and if an army crossed, it still would have to get to Richmond. Northwest (and much nearer west than north) of the city, the Rappahannock is fordable, but its course is *away* from Richmond, and the roads to Richmond *again lead back toward the rear of Fredericksburg.*

There were, therefore, but two feasible plans for the North to accomplish its "on to Richmond" purpose. One was to take Fredericksburg and with it the roads and railway to Richmond; Burnside tried this. The other, to cross the river just above, and get in the rear of Fredericksburg, thus getting the roads and railways to Richmond; Hooker and Grant tried this.

On November 20th, General Sumner peremptorily demanded the surrender of the town, under threat of immediate bombardment, but on receiving a request from Mayor Slaughter, he consented to extend the time twenty-four hours and sent General Patrick across the river with a message, as follows:

"Gentlemen: Under cover of the houses of your town, shots have been fired upon the troops of my command. Your mills and factories are furnishing provisions and materials for clothing for armed bodies in rebellion against the authority of the Government of the United States. Your railroads and other means of transportation are removing supplies to the depot of such troops. This condition of things must terminate; and by direction of Major-General Burnside, commanding this army, I accordingly demand the surrender of this city into my hands, as a representative of the Government of the United States, at or before five o'clock this afternoon (five o'clock P. M. to-day). Failing an affirmative reply to this demand by the time indicated, sixteen hours will be permitted to elapse for the removal from the city of women and children, the sick, wounded, and aged; which period having elapsed, I shall proceed to shell the town.

The Citizens Driven Out

"Upon obtaining possession of the town, every necessary means will be taken to preserve order and to secure the protective operation of the laws and policy of the United States Government."

While General Patrick waited from 10:00 A. M. until 7:00 P. M. (November 21) in a log house at French John's Wharf, the note was passed through the hands of a civic committee who had previously met General Lee at "Snowden," (now the beautiful home of Mr. and Mrs. F. C. Baldwin) on which were: Mayor Slaughter, William A. Little and Douglas H. Gordon. A note from General Lee was then transmitted to the town officials by General J. E. B. Stuart. This Mayor Slaughter, Dr. Wm. S. Scott and Samuel Harrison delivered late in the afternoon to General Patrick. General Lee simply said the town was non-combatant; that he would not occupy it, nor would he allow any one else to occupy it.

Advised by General Lee, the inhabitants of the town now began to refugee to the rear. They went in the dark, in a snow storm, afoot, in vehicles and some in a railway train, upon which the Northern guns opened heavy fire. They slept in barns, cabins and the homes of country people, and left behind their silverware and fine old china, their paintings and portraits and every kind of property, all of which was doomed to destruction.

But the town was not shelled and a few at a time many of the old men and the women, the boys and girls, crept back from impossible shelters in the country to their homes in the town.

Then, twenty-two days later, at dawn of December 11th, at a signal from the "Long Tom" on Scott's Hill, at Falmouth, Burnside opened on the town, now half full of residents, with one hundred and eighty-one guns. The guns were placed along Stafford Heights from the Washington Farm to Falmouth, and the whole fire was concentrated on the town, where walls toppled, fires sprang up and chaos reigned.

Frequently the Union gunners fired a hundred guns a minute, round shot, case shot and shell. The quick puffs of smoke, touched in the center with flame, ran incessantly along the hills and a vast thunder echoed thirty miles away. Soon the town was under a pall of smoke, through which lifted the white spires of the churches.

"The scenes following the bombardment," says John Esten Cooke, in "Jackson," "were cruel. Men, women and children were driven from town. Hundreds of ladies and children were seen wandering homeless over the frozen highways, with bare feet and thin clothing. Delicately nurtured girls walked hurriedly over the various roads, seeking some friendly roof to cover them."

The following article by one who, as a little girl, was in Fredericksburg on the day of the bombardment, catches a glimpse of it in a personal way that is more convincing than pages of description.

THE SHELLING OF FREDERICKSBURG

Recollections of Mrs Frances Bernard Goolrick (Mrs. John T. Goolrick) who was a little girl at that time.

During the stormy winter of 1862, my mother, a widow with three little children, was still in her native place, Fredericksburg, Virginia. Many of the inhabitants had long since left for Richmond and other points farther south, for the town lying just between the hostile armies was the constant scene of raids and skirmishes, and no one knew at what instant everything might be swept away from them. My mother, separated from her relatives by the fortunes of war, decided that it would be best for her to remain where she was and thus probably save the household effects she had gathered around her. The strongest arguments had been used by friends in town and relatives at a distance to induce her to leave for a place of more safety, but so far without avail, and though we were often alarmed by raids into town, as yet we had sustained no injuries of any description. In the fall the Federal army, under General Burnside, was on the Stafford hills just across the river, and it was constantly rumored that the town would be bombarded; but lulled to an insecure rest by many false alarms, the people had but little faith in these rumors.

* * * * * * * * *

On the 11th of December, one of the most cruel and heartless acts of the war was to be perpetrated, the town of Fredericksburg was bombarded, the roar of guns beginning at daybreak, with no one in it but old or invalid men and helpless women and children. As quick as thought, we were up and dressed, and my aunt being very rapid in her movements, was the first to reach the cellar. My mother had long since had some chairs and other pieces of furniture placed there in case of an emergency. I being the first child dressed, ran out into the yard, and as I turned towards the cellar steps I beheld, it seemed to me, the most brilliant light that I had ever seen; as I looked, my aunt reached out her arms and pulled me, quivering with terror, into the cellar. A shell had exploded at the back of the garden, in reality at some distance, but to me it was as if it had been at my very feet. The family soon assembled, including the servants; we had also additions in the way of two gentlemen from Stafford, Mr. B. and Mr. G., who had been detained in town, and a Lieutenant Eustace, of Braxton's battery, who was returning from a visit to his home. Also a colored family, Uncle Charles and Aunt Judy, with a small boy named Douglas and two or three other children. The couple had been left in charge of their mistress' home (she being out of town), and with no cellar to their house they were fain to come into ours.

And now the work of destruction began, and for long hours the only sounds that greeted our ears were the whizzing and moaning of the shells and the crash of falling bricks and timber. My mother and we three children were seated on a

Hiding From The Shells

low bed with Ca'line, a very small darkey, huddled as close to us children as she could get, trying to keep warm. Mr B. and Mr. G. occupied positions of honor on each side of the large old-fashioned fire-place, while my aunt was cowering inside, and every time a ball would roll through the house or a shell explode, she would draw herself up and moan and shiver. Lieutenant Eustace was a great comfort to my mother, and having some one to rely on enabled her to keep her courage up during the terrible ordeal of the cannonading. Although my brother, sister and myself were all frightened, we could not help laughing at the little darkey children who were positively stricken dumb with terror, old Aunt Judy keeping them close to her side and giving them severe cuffs and bangs if they moved so much as a finger.

My aunt, as well as the rest of us, now began to feel the pangs of hunger, and Aunt B. ordered the cook in the most positive manner to go up to the kitchen and make some coffee, telling her that she knew she was afraid and we would all be satisfied with only a cup of coffee for the present. I believe Aunt Sally would have gone without a word if my mother had told her, but this, from an outsider, she could not bear. (Aunt B. was my uncle's wife and the family servants had seen very little of her.) She, therefore, demurred, and Aunt B. calling her a coward, she arose in a perfect fury, and with insubordination written upon her from her rigid backbone to her flashing eyes, informed Aunt B. "dat she warn no mo' a coward dan de res' of 'em, but she didn't b'lieve Mars Gen'l Lee hisself cud stan' up making coffee under dat tornady." Just about this time Uncle Charles sprawled himself out upon the floor in ungovernable terror, and called upon the Lord to save him and his family. "Pray for us all, Uncle Charles," screamed my aunt, her voice just heard above the roar of artillery. The cannonading was now something fearful. Our house had been struck twice and the shrieking balls and bursting bombs were enough to appall the stoutest heart. My aunt being brave in speech, but in reality very timorous, and Uncle Charles "a bright and shining light" among the colored persuasion, she again requested him to pray. Aunt Judy by this time began to bewail that she had "lef' old Miss cow in the cowshed," and mistaking the moaning of the shells for the dying groans of the cow, she and Douglas lamented it in true darkey fashion. Uncle Charles meanwhile was very willing to pray, but Aunt Judy objected strenuously, saying, "dis ain't no time to be spendin' in pra'ar, Char's Pryor, wid dem bumb shells flying over you and a fizzlin' around you, and ole Miss cow dyin' right dar in your sight." But when the house was struck for the third time, Aunt B., in despairing accents, begged Uncle Charles to pray, so he fell upon his knees by an old barrel, in the middle of the cellar floor, upon which sat a solitary candle, whose flickering light lit up his hushed and solemn countenance, and in tremulous tones with many interjections, offered up a prayer.

* * * * * * * * *

My mother thought of my father's portrait, and afraid of its being injured she determined to get it herself, and bring it into the cellar. Without telling anyone of her intentions, she left the cellar and went up into the parlor; the portrait was hanging just over a sofa, on which she stood to take it down. She had just reached the door opposite the sofa when a shell came crashing through the wall, demolishing the sofa on which she had so recently stood, as well as many other articles of furniture. She reached the cellar, white and trembling, but with the portrait unhurt in her arms.

At one o'clock the cannonading suddenly ceased and for one hour we were at liberty to go above and see the damage that had been done. My mother's first efforts were directed towards getting a lunch, of which we were all sorely in need. With the aid of one of the frightened servants she succeeded in getting a fire and having some coffee made and with this, together with some cold bread and ham, we had a plentiful repast.

What a scene met our eyes; our pretty garden was strewn with cannon balls and pieces of broken shells, limbs knocked

"Refugeeing" in Winter

off the trees and the grape arbor a perfect wreck. The house had been damaged considerably, several large holes torn through it, both in front and back. While we were deploring the damage that had been done, Lieutenant Eustace returned in breathless haste to say that he had just heard an order from General Lee read on Commerce Street, saying that the women and children must leave town, as he would destroy it with hot shell that night, sooner than let it fall into the hands of the enemy, who were rapidly crossing the river on pontoon bridges. They urged my mother to take her children and fly at once from the town. After resisting until the gentlemen in despair were almost ready to drag her from her dangerous situation, she finally consented to leave. The wildest confusion now reigned, the servants wringing their hands and declaring they could not go without their "Chists," which they all managed to get somehow, and put upon their heads, but the gentlemen insisted so that we had only time to save our lives. They would not even let my mother go back into the house to get her purse or a single valuable. So we started just as we were; my wrapping, I remember, was an old ironing blanket, with a large hole burnt in the middle. I never did find out whether Aunt B. ever got her clothes on, for she stalked ahead of us, wrapped in a pure white counterpane, a tall, ghostly looking figure, who seemed to glide with incredible rapidity over the frozen ground. * * *

We plodded along under a heavy cross fire, balls falling right and left of us. We left the town by way of the old "plank road," batteries of Confederates on both sides. The ground was rough and broken up by the tramping of soldiers and the heavy wagons and artillery that had passed over it, so that it was difficult and tiresome to walk, and the sun got warm by this time and the snow was melting rapidly; the mud was indescribable."

We had now reached the "Reservoir," a wooden building over "Poplar Spring," and about a mile from town. I had already lost one of my shoes several times, because of having

Pillage and Plunder

no string in it, and my little brother insisted on giving me one of his, so we sat down by the "Reservoir" feeling very secure, but were terribly alarmed in a few moments by a ball coming through the building and whizzing very close to our ears. No, this would not do, so on we went, footsore and weary; sometimes we would meet a soldier who would carry one of us a short distance. All of our servants, except Ca'line, who was only seven years old, had taken some other direction. When we got about two miles from town we overtook many other refugees; some were camping by the way, and others pressing on, some to country houses which were hospitably thrown open to wanderers from home, and others to "Salem Church," about three miles from Fredericksburg, where there was a large encampment. Our destination was a house not far from "Salem Church," which we now call the "Refuge House." Exhausted, we reached the house by twilight, found there some friends who had been there some weeks, and who kindly took us into their room and gave us every attention. And so great was our relief to feel that we had escaped from the horror of that day, that such small matters as having to sleep in the room with a dozen people, having no milk and no coffee, our principal diet consisting of corn bread, bacon and sorghum, seemed only slight troubles."

* * * * * * * * *

From the end of the bombardment, and at the first invasion of the town by Union forces, until they were driven across the river again, Fredericksburg was mercilessly sacked. All day, from the houses, and particularly from the grand old homes that distinguished the town, came the noise of splintering furniture, the crash of chinaware, and — now and then — a scream. On the walls hung headless portraits, the face gashed by bayonets. Bayonets ripped open mattresses and the feathers heaped in piles or blew about the streets, littered with women's and men's clothing and letters and papers thrown out of desks. Mahogany furniture warmed the despoilers, and ten thousand were drunk on pilfered liquors. Windows and doors were smashed, the streets full of debris,

THE CONFEDERATE CEMETERY

In the Lower Left Corner the Plank Road and Marye's Heights

A Carnival of Horrors

through which drunken men grotesquely garbed in women's shawls and bonnets, staggered; flames rose in smoke pillars here and there, and the provost guard was helpless to control the strange orgy of stragglers and camp followers who were wild with plunder lust, amid the dead and wounded strewn about. A fearful picture of war was Fredericksburg in those December days from the eleventh to the thirteenth.

To the citizens of Fredericksburg, those days meant bankruptcy, for their slaves walked away, their stores and churches were battered, their silverware stolen, their homes despoiled and their clothing worn or thrown away. Wealthy men were to walk back a few days later to their home town as paupers; women and children were to come back to hunger and discomfort in bleak winter weather; and all this was the result of what General Lee said was an entirely "unnecessary" bombardment and of days of pillage, which no earnest attempt to stop was made. Fredericksburg was the blackest spot on Burnside's none too effulgent reputation.

From the army, from Southern cities and from individuals money for relief came liberally, and in all nearly $170,000. was contributed to aid in feeding, clothing and making habitable homes for the unfortunate town's people. A good many carloads of food came, too, but the whole barely relieved the worst misery, for the $170,000. was Confederate money, with its purchasing power at low mark.

The First Battle

At Mayre's Heights and Hamilton's Crossing, war claimed her sacrifice

Following the shelling of Fredericksburg, on December 11th, the Union army began to cross on pontoons. On the 12th of December, under cover of the guns and of fog, almost the whole Union army crossed on three pontoons, one near the foot of Hawk street, another just above the car bridge, and one at Deep Run. On the morning of December 13th, General Burnside's army was drawn up in a line of battle from opposite Falmouth to Deep Run. It was, say they who saw the vast army with artillery and cavalry advanced, banners flying and the bayonets of their infantry hosts gleaming as the fog lifted, one of the most imposing sights of the war.

General Burnside actually had in line and fought during the day, according to his report, 100,000 effective men.

General Lee had 57,000 effectives, ranged along the hills from Taylors, past Snowden, past Marye's Heights, past Hazel Run and on to Hamilton's Crossing.

There were preliminary skirmishes of cavalry, light artillery and infantry. The enemy tried to "feel" General Lee's lines.

Then, about 10 o'clock, they advanced against the hills near Hamilton's Crossing, where Jackson's Corps was posted, in a terrific charge across a broad plateau between the river and the hills to within a quarter of a mile of the Confederate position, where they broke under terrific artillery and musketry fire. At one o'clock 55,000 men, the whole of Franklin's and Hooker's Grand Divisions advanced again in the mightiest single charge of the Civil War. Stuart and Pelham (he earned that day from Lee the title of "The Gallant Pelham") raked them with light artillery, but nevertheless they forced a wedge through Jackson's lines and had won the day, until Jackson's reserves, thrown into the breach, drove them out and threw

At Hamilton's Crossing

back the whole line. As dusk came on, Stuart and Pelham counter charged, advancing their guns almost to the Bowling Green road, and Jackson prepared to charge and "drive them into the river," but was stopped by the heavy Union guns on Stafford hills.

During the fiercest part of the battle, "Stonewall" Jackson was on the hill just on the Fredericksburg side of Hamilton's Crossing where Walker's artillery was posted, but toward evening, fired with his hope of driving the Union forces across the river, he rode rapidly from place to place, sending out frequent orders. One of these he gave to an aide.

"Captain, go through there and if you and your horse come out alive, tell Stuart I am going to advance my whole line at sunset." It was this charge, mentioned above, which failed.

Late that night, rising from the blankets which he shared with a Chaplain, Jackson wrote some orders. While he was doing this, an orderly came and standing at the tent flap, said, "General Gregg is dying, General, and sent me to say to you that he wrote you a letter recently in which he used expressions he is sorry for. He says he meant no disrespect by that letter and was only doing what he thought was his duty. He hopes you will forgive him."

Without hesitation, Jackson, who was deeply stirred, answered, "Tell General Gregg I will be with him directly."

He rode through the woods back to where the brave Georgian was dying, and day was about to break when he came back to his troops.

General Maxey Gregg, of Georgia, was killed in action here, as were a number of other gallant officers.

Jackson held the right of the Confederate lines all day with 26,000 men against 55,000. His losses were about 3,415, while Hooker and Franklin lost 4,447. Meanwhile, against Marye's Heights, the left center of the line, almost two miles away, General Burnside sent again and again terrific infantry charges.

The Charge at Marye's Heights

The hills just back of Fredericksburg are fronted by an upward sloping plane, and at the foot of that part of the hills called Marye's Heights is a stone wall and the "Sunken Road"—as fatal here for Burnside as was the Sunken Road at Waterloo for Napoleon. On Marye's Heights was the Washington Artillery, and a number of guns — a veritable fortress, ready, as General Pegram said, "to sweep the plains in front as close as a fine-tooth comb." At the foot of the heights behind the stone wall were Gen. Cooke's and Gen. Cobb's brigades, Kershaw's South Carolinians, and Ransom's North Carolinians—nine thousand riflemen, six deep, firing over the front lines' shoulders, so that, so one officer wrote "they literally sent bullets in sheets."

Against this impregnable place, Burnside launched charge after charge. and never did men go more bravely and certainly to death. This was simultaneous with the fighting at Hamilton's Crossing.

Meagher's Irish Brigade went first across the plain. Detouring from Hanover street and George street, they formed line of battle on the lowest ground, and with cedar branches waving in their hats, bravely green in memory of "the ould sod" they swept forward until the rifles behind the wall and the cannon on the hill decimated their ranks; and yet again they formed and charged, until over the whole plain lay the dead, with green cedar boughs waving idly in their hats. The Irish Brigade was practically exterminated, and three more charges by larger bodies failed, although one Northern officer fell within twenty-five yards of the wall. The day ended in the utter defeat of the Union Army, which withdrew into Fredericksburg at night.

In front of the wall 8,217 Union soldiers were killed or wounded, and in the "Sunken Road" the Confederates lost 1,962.

The total Union loss in the whole battle of Fredericksburg was 12,664 and the Confederates' loss 5,377.

General J. R. Cooke, of the Confederate Army, was wounded almost at the moment Cobb fell. General C. F.

The Death of General Cobb

Jackson and General Bayard, of the Union Army, were killed, the latter dying in the Bernard House, "Mansfield," where Franklin had his headquarters.

General T. R. R. Cobb, the gallant commander of the Georgians, fell mortally wounded at the stone wall, and tradition has said that he was killed by a shell fired from the lawn of his mother's home, a dramatic story that is refuted by evidence that he was killed by a sharpshooter in a house at the left and in front of the "Sunken Road."

But the brilliant Georgian, who aided in formulating the Confederate Constitution, was killed within sight of the house, where, more than forty years before, the elder Cobb met, and in which he married, her who was to be the General's mother. Journeying late in 1819 North to attend Congress, Senator John Forsythe, who was born in Fredericksburg, and Senator Cobb, Sr., were guests of Thomas R. Rootes, Esq., at Federal Hill, a great house that sits at the edge of the town, overlooking the little valley and Marye's Heights, and there began a romance that led to marriage of Miss Rootes and Senator Cobb, in the mansion, in 1820. From the spot where he stood when he died, had not the smoke of a terrific battle screened it, their son, the Georgian General, could have clearly seen the windows of the room in which his parents were married.

General Cobb died in the yard of a small house, just at the edge of the "Sunken Road," ministered to in his last moments, as was many another man who drank the last bitter cup that day, by an angel of mercy and a woman of dauntless courage, Mrs. Martha Stevens.

Her house was in the center of the fire, yet she refused to leave it, and there between the lines, with the charges rolling up to her yard fence and tons of lead shrieking about her, Mrs. Stevens stayed all day, giving the wounded drink, and bandaging their wounds until every sheet and piece of clothing in the house had been used to bind a soldier's hurts. At times the fire of Northern troops was concentrated on her house so that General Lee, frowning, turned to those about him and said: "I wish those people would let Mrs. Stevens alone."

Lee Spares Old "Chatham"

Nothing in the war was finer than the spirit of this woman, who stayed between the lines in and about her house, through the planks of which now and then a bullet splintered its way, miraculouly living in a hail of missiles where, it seemed, nothing else could live.

During the battle at Fredericksburg, General Lee stood on "Lee's Hill," an eminence near Hazel Run, and between Marye's Heights and Hamilton's crossing. Looking across the Rappahannock he could see "Chatham," the great winged brick house where General Burnside had headquarters, and where, under the wide spreading oaks, General Lee had won his bride, the pretty Mary Custis. The fine old place was now the property of Major Lacy, who rode up to Lee and said: "General there are a group of Yankee officers on my porch. I do not want my house spared. I ask permission to give orders to shell it." General Lee, smiling, said: "Major, I do not want to shell your fine old house. Besides, it has tender memories for me. I courted my bride under its trees."

In all this saturnalia of blood, it is a relief to find something in lighter vein, and in this case it is furnished by two Irishmen, Meagher and Mitchell. This little incident takes us back some years to "Ould Ireland." Here three young Irishmen, Charles Francis Meagher, John Boyle O'Reily and John Mitchell, known respectively, as the Irish Orater, Poet and Patriot, fired by love for Free Ireland and Home Rule, earned exile for themselves and left Ireland hurriedly. O'Reily settled in Boston and became a well-known poet and a champion of the North. Meagher settled in New York, and at the outbreak of the War organized the Irish Brigade, of which he was made Brigadier-General. Mitchell settled in Richmond, where he became the editor of the Richmond Enquirer, and, as a spectator, stood on Marye's Heights during the battle and witnessed the desperate charges and bloody repulses of his old friend, Meagher; and as he watched he unburdened his soul. His refrain varied between exultation at the sight of a fine fight and execration, in picturesque and

BROMPTON, ON MARYE'S HEIGHTS; THE STONE WALL.
Where Terrible Charges Spent Themselves. Sunken Road is in Foreground. Residence of Capt. M. B. Rowe.

The Good Samaritan

satisfying language, of the "renegade Irishman," his one-time friend, who would fight against the very principle, the advocacy of which had brought them exile from Ireland.

Mitchell's grandson was John Purroy Mitchell, mayor of New York City, who died in the Aviation service during the late war.

There was another soul at the Battle of Fredericksburg whose spirit of mercy to the suffering was stronger than the dread of death, and in the Chapel of the Prince of Peace at Gettysburg, is a tablet to him, Dick Kirkland — the "Angel of Maryes' Heights"— a gracious memorial placed by the Federal survivors of that fight.

Dick Kirkland, a Southern soldier, who all day long had fought behind the Stone Wall, laid aside all animosity when night fell and the bitter cries arose in the chill air from the wounded and dying on the plain. The pitiful calls for "water, water" so moved the young South Carolinian that he asked his commanding officer to be allowed to relieve the sufferers. His request was at first refused, but when he begged, permission was given, and taking as many full canteens as he could carry, he went out among the pitiful forms dotting the field, while the shells and rifle fire still made it most dangerous, administering to the enemy. He was a good Samaritan and unafraid, who is affectionately remembered by a grateful foe. Kirkland was more merciful to the wounded Federals than was their commander, for it was forty-eight hours before General Burnside could swallow his pride and acknowledge defeat by applying for a truce. In the interval, during forty-eight hours of winter weather while the wounded lay unsheltered, chill winds sweeping over them, the wailing and the agonized crying slowly died out. Every wounded man who could not crawl or walk died, and when the truce came more than four thousand bodies were piled in front of the "Sunken Road."

At night of December 13th, Burnside was utterly defeated and after quietly facing the Southern forces all day on the 14th, he was practically forced to abandon his battle plans by the protests of his Generals, who practically refused to charge again, and moved his army across the river at night.

In the whole action at Fredericksburg, General Lee used but 57,000 men, while official reports state that the Norhern forces "in the fight" numbered 100,000 As bearing on this (and most assuredly with no intention to belittle the gallant men of the Federal Army, who fought so bravely) the condition of Burnside's Army, due to the policy of his government and to Major-General Hooker's insubordination, is to be considered. An estimate of this army by the New York Times shows to what pass vacillation had brought it. The Times said after Fredericksburg.

"Sad, sad it is to look at this suberb Army of the Potomac — the match of which no conqueror ever led — this incomparable army, fit to perform the mission the country has imposed upon it — paralyzed, petrified, put under a blight and a spell. You see men who tell you that they have been in a dozen battles and have been licked and chased every time — they would like to chase once to see how it "feels." This begins to tell on them. Their splendid qualities, their patience, faith, hope and courage, are gradually oozing out. Certainly never were a graver, gloomier, more sober, sombre, serious and unmusical body of men than the Army of the Potomac at the present time."

On the other hand, thus spoke the correspondent of the London Times of the "tatterdermalion regiments of the South":

"It is a strange thing to look at these men, so ragged, slovenly, sleeveless, without a superfluous ounce of flesh on their bones, with wild, matted hair, in mendicants rags, and to think, when the battle flags go to the front, how they can and do fight. 'There is only one attitude in which I should never be ashamed of you seeing my men, and that is when they are fighting.' These were General Lee's words to me the first time I ever saw him."

At Chancellorsville

The Struggle in the Pine Woods when death struck at Southern hearts

From the close of the battle at Fredericksburg in December 1862, until the spring of 1863, General Burnside's Army of the Potomac and General Lee's Army of Northern Virginia lay in camp; the first on the north and the second on the south bank of the Rappahannock. The little town, now fairly well repopulated by returned refugees, lay between the hosts. The Northern lines practically began at Falmouth, where General Daniel Butterfield had headquarters, and at which spot young Count Zeppelin and his assistants were busily arranging to send up a great Observation Balloon with a signalling outfit. Southward, Lee's army stretched over thirty-three miles, from the fords of the Rappahannock, where the hard riding cavalrymen of Stuart and W. H. F. Lee watched, to Port Royal, Jackson's right.

Burnside's headquarters were the Phillips house and Chatham, (recently owned by the famous journalist, Mark Sullivan and where he and Mrs. Sullivan made their home for some years). Hooker, part of the time, was at the Phillips house, Lee in a tent, near Fredericksburg, while General Jackson had headquarters first in an outbuilding at Moss Neck, now the home of Count d'Adhemar and later in a tent. It was here that he became fond of little Farley Corbin, who came every day to perch on his knee and receive little presents from him. One day he had nothing to give her, and so, ere she left, he tore the gold braid from the new hat that was part of a handsome uniform just given him by General "Jeb" Stuart, and placed it like a garland on her pretty curly head. During the winter the General, who from the beginning of the war never slept at night outside his army's camp, nor had an honr's leave of absence, saw for the first time since he left Lexington, and for next to the last time on earth, his wife and little daughter, whom he so fervently loved. They spent some weeks near him at Moss Neck.

Christmas Eve came. In the Southern camp back of the hills down the river road, up towards Banks Ford, out at Salem Church, and even in the town, hunger and cold were the lot of all. General Lee, wincing at the sufferings of his "tatterdermalion" forces, wrote and asked that the rations of his men be increased, but a doctor-inspector sent out by the often futile Confederate Government reported that the bacon ration of Lee's army — one-half a pound a day, might be cut down, as "the men can be *kept alive* on this." General Lee himself wrote that his soldiers were eating berries, leaves, roots and the bark of trees to "supplement the ration," and although at this time the Confederate Government had a store of bacon and corn meal that would have fed *all* its armies a half year, Lee's ragged soldiers starved throughout the winter. It is worthy of note here that when Lee's starving army moved, foodless, toward that last day at Appomattox, they marched past 50,000 pounds of bacon alone, which the Confederate commissary, at Mr. Jefferson Davis' orders, burned next day.

We spoke of Christmas Eve, when in the long lines of the two camps great fires beamed, voices rose in songs and hymns, and bands played. Late in the evening, when dusk had settled, a band near Brompton broke out defiantly into "Dixie," and from the Washington Farm a big band roared out "The Battle Hymn." There was a pause and then, almost simultaneously, they began "Home, Sweet Home," and catching the time played it through together. When it was done, up from the camps of these boys who were to kill and be killed, who were to die in misery on many a sodden field, rose a wild cheer.

Hardly could two great armies ever before have lain for months within sight of each other as these two did in almost amicable relations. There was no firing; the cannon-crowned hills were silent. Drills and great reviews took place on either bank of the river and in the Confederate ranks there went on a great religious "revival" that swept through the organization.

The Coming of Spring

Along the banks of the river where pickets patrolled by day, and their little fires flamed in the night, trading was active. From the Union bank would come the call softly:

"Johnny."
"Yea, Yank."
"Got any tobacco?"
"Yes, want 't trade?"
"Half pound of coffee for two plugs of tobacco, Reb."
" 'right, send 'er over."

They traded coffee, tobacco, newspapers and provisions, sometimes wading out and meeting in mid-river, but as the industry grew, miniature ferry lines, operated by strings, began to ply.

Soldiers and Generals passed and repassed in the streets of Fredericksburg, where wreckage still lay about in confusion, houses presented dilapidated fronts, and only a few of the citizens attempted to occupy their homes.

Once, in midwinter, the armies became active when Burnside attempted to move his army and cross the river above Fredericksburg; but only for a few days, for that unfortunate General's plans were ruined by a deluge and his army "stuck in the mud." General Hooker took his place.

About April 26 Hooker's great army, "The finest army on the planet," he bombastically called it, moved up the river and began crossing. It was his purpose to get behind Lee's lines, surprise him and defeat him from the rear. On April twenty-ninth and thirtieth, Hooker got in position around Chancellorsville, in strong entrenchments, a part of his army amounting to 85,000 men, but the Confederate skirmishers were already in front of him.

It was the Northern Commander's plan for Sedgwick, left at Fredericksburg with 40,000, to drive past Fredericksburg and on to Chancellorsville, and thus to place the Southern forces between the two big Federal armies and crush it.

The First Aerial Scout

Before the great battle of Chancellorsville began, this message came down from the first balloon ever successfully used in war, tugging at its cable two thousand feet above the Scott house, on Falmouth Heights:

Balloon in the Air, April 29, 1863.
Major-General Butterfield,
 Chief of Staff, Army of the Potomac.

General: The enemy's line of battle is formed in the edge of the woods, at the foot of the heights, from opposite Fredericksburg to some distance to the left of our lower crossing. Their line appears quite thin, compared with our forces. Their tents all remain as heretofore, as far as I can see.

T. C. S. LOWE,
Chief of Aeronauts.

But the force did not "remain as heretofore" long, though the tents were left to confuse the enemy, for on April 29 General Anderson moved to Chancellorsville, followed on April 30 by General McLaws; and under cover of darkness "Stonewall Jackson" moved to the same place that night, with 26,000 men. On May 1, then, Hooker's 91,000 at Chancellorsville were being pressed by Lee's army of 46,000.

General Early's command of 9,000 and Barksdale's brigade of 1,000 and some detached troops were left to defend Fredericksburg against Sedgwick's corps, which was now crossing the Rappahannock, 30,000 strong. At 11 A. M., May 1, General Lee's army, with Jackson's corps on his left, began the attack at Chancellorsville, of which this dispatch speaks:

Balloon in the Air, May 1, 1863.
Major-General Sedgwick,
 Commanding Left Wing, Army of the Potomac.

General: In a northwest direction, about twelve miles, an engagement is going on.

T. C. S. LOWE,
Chief of Aeronauts.

Fight at Chancellorsville

Before evening of May 1 Hooker's advance guard was driven back, and the Confederate forces swept on until within one mile of Chancellorsville, and there, stopped by a "position of great natural strength" (General Lee) and by deep entrenchments, log breastworks and felled trees, they ceased to progress. It was evident at nightfall that with his inferior force the Southern commander could not drive Hooker, and that if he failed to do so, Sedgwick would drive back the small force in Fredericksburg and would come on from Fredericksburg and crush him.

Jackson and Lee bivouaced that night near where the Old Plank Road and the Furnace Road intersect, and here formulated their plans for the morrow. From Captain Murray Taylor, of General A. P. Hill's staff, they learned that by advancing down the Furnace Road southward, then turning sharply and marching in a "V" on Brock Road marching northward, Jackson's plan to turn Hooker's right might be carried out, and at Captain Taylor's suggestion they sent for "Jack" Hayden, who could not be gotten at once, and who, being an old man, was "hiding out" to avoid "Yankee" marauders.

Lee and Jackson slept on the ground. Jackson, over whom an officer had thrown his overcoat, despite his protests, waited until the officer dozed, gently laid the coat over him and slept uncovered, as he had not brought his own overcoat. Later, arising chilled, he sat by the fire until near dawn, when his army got in motion.

When Jackson moved away in the early hours of May 2 there were left to face Hooker's 91,000 men on the Federal left, Lee's 14,000 men, attacking and feinting, and nowhere else a man. Jackson was moving through tangled forests, over unused roads, and before 5 o'clock of that memorable afternoon of May 2 he had performed the never-equalled feat of moving an army, infantry and artillery of 26,000 men sixteen miles, entirely around the enemy, and reversing his own army's front. He was now across the Plank Road and

Jackson's Stroke of Genius

the Turnpike, about four miles from Chancellorsville, facing toward Lee's line, six miles away. And Hooker was between them!

It was 5:30 when Jackson's command (Colston's and Rhodes' Divisions, with A. P. Hill in reserve) gave forth the rebel yell and sweeping along through the woods parallel to the roads, fell on Hooker's right while the unsuspecting army was at supper. The Federals fled in utter disorder.

Before his victorious command, Jackson drove Hooker's army through the dark pine thickets until the Federal left had fallen on Chancellorsville and the right wing was piled up and the wagon trains fleeing, throwing the whole retreating army into confusion. At 9 o'clock he held some of the roads in Hooker's rear, and the Northern army was in his grasp.

Hill was to go forward now. He rode to the front with his staff, a short distance behind Jackson, who went a hundred yards ahead of the Confederate lines on the turnpike to investigate. Bullets suddenly came singing from the Northern lines and Jackson turned and rode back to his own lines. Suddenly a Confederate picket shouted "Yankee cavalry," as he rode through the trees along the edge of the Plank Road. Then a volley from somewhere in Lane's North Carolina ranks poured out, and three bullets struck Jackson in the hand and arm. His horse bolted, but was stopped and turned, and Jackson was aided by General Hill to dismount. Almost all of Hill's staff were killed or wounded.

There was trouble getting a litter, and the wounded man tried to walk, leaning on Major Leigh and Lieutenant James Power Smith. The road was filled with men, wounded, retreating, lost from their commands. Hill's lines were forming for a charge and from these Jackson hid his face — they must not know he was wounded. A litter was brought and they bore the sufferer through the thickets until a fusilade passed about them and struck down a litter-bearer, so that the General was thrown from the litter his crushed shoulder striking a pine stump, and now for the first time, and last time, he groaned. Again they

Where "Stonewall Jackson" Died

In the Room on the Lower Floor, the Window of Which Looks Out on the Little Bush, The South's Hero Passed Away

The Death of "Stonewall"

bore him along the Plank Road until a gun loaded with canister swept that road clear, and the litter-bearers fled, leaving General Jackson lying in the road. And here, with infinite heroism, Lieutenant Smith (see sketch of life) and Major Leigh lay with their bodies over him to shield him from missiles.

Later the wounded officer was gotten to a field headquarters near Wilderness Run, and Dr. Hunter McGuire and assistants amputated one arm and bound the other arm and hand. Two days later he was removed to Mr. Chandler's home, near Guineas, where, refusing to enter the mansion because he feared his presence might bring trouble on the occupants should the Federals come, and because the house was crowded with other wounded, he was placed in a small outbuilding, which stands today. The record of his battle against death in this little cabin, his marvelous trust in God and his uncomplaining days of suffering until he opened his lips to feebly say: "Let us pass over the river and rest under the shade of the trees" is a beautiful story in itself. He died May 10th, 1863, from pneumonia, which developed when his wounds were beginning to heal. The wounds only would not have killed him and the pneumonia probably resulted from sleeping uncovered on the night before referred to. Mrs. Jackson and their little child, Dr. Hunter McGuire, Lieutenant James Power Smith, his aide-de-camp; Mrs. Beasley and a negro servant were those closest to him in his dying hours.

Hill succeeded Jackson, and in twenty minutes was wounded and Stuart succeeded him, and fighting ceased for the night.

On May 3, General Lee attacked again, uniting his left wing with Stuart's right, and a terrific battle took place that lasted all day, and at its end Hooker's great army was defeated and dispirited, barely holding on in their third line trenches, close to the river; that worse did not befall him was due to events about Fredericksburg. (We may note here that Hooker lost at Chancellorsville 16,751 men while Lee lost about 11,000.)

Battle at Salem Church

For Sedgwick, with 30,000 men, took Marye's Heights at 1 o'clock of this day, losing about 1,000 men, and immediately General Brooks' division (10,000) marchd out the Plank Road, where on each successive crest, Wilcox's Alabamians, with a Virginia battery of two guns (4,000 in all) disputed the way. At Salem Church, General Wilcox planted his troops for a final stand.

Here at Salem Church the battle began when Sedgwick's advance guard, beating its way all day against a handful of Confederates, finally formed late in the afternoon of May 3, prepared to throw their column in a grand assault against the few Confederates standing sullenly on the pine ridge which crosses the Plank Road at right angles about where Salem Church stands. Less than 4,000 Alabama troops, under General Wilcox, held the line, and against these General Brooks, of Sedgwick's corps, threw his 10,000 men. They rushed across the slopes, met in the thicket, and here they fought desperately for an hour. Reinforcements reached the Confederates at sundown, and next morning General Lee had come with Anderson's and McLaw's commands, and met nearly the whole of Sedgwick's command, charging them late in the afternoon of May 4, and driving them so that, before daybreak, they had retreated across the river. Then, turning back to attack Hooker, he found the latter also crossing the river.

Unique in the history of battles are the two monuments which stand near Salem Church, erected by the State of New Jersey and gallantly uttering praise of friend and foe.

They mark the farthest advance of the New Jersey troops. The first, on the right of the Plank Road as one goes from Fredericksburg to Chancellorsville, is a monument to the Fifteenth New Jersey troops, and one one side is inscribed:

"The survivors of the Fifteenth New Jersey Infantry honor their comrades who bore themselves bravely in this contest, and bear witness to the valor of the men who opposed them on this field."

Monument at Salem Church

The other monument stands on the ridge at Salem Church, close to the road, and about where the charge of the Twenty-third New Jersey shattered itself against the thin lines of Wilcox's Alabamians. It stands just where these two bodies of troops fought hand to hand amidst a rolling fire of musketry, bathing the ground in blood. In the end the Confederates prevailed, but when the State of New Jersey erected the monument they did not forget their foe. It is the only monument on a battlefield that pays homage alike to friend and enemy.

The monument was unveiled in 1907, Governor E. Bird Gubb, who led the Twenty-third New Jersey, being the principal speaker. Thousands were present at the ceremonies.

On one side of the splendid granite shaft is a tablet, on which is engraved:

"To the memory of our heroic comrades who gave their lives for their country's unity on this battlefield, this tablet is dedicated."

And on the other side another tablet is inscribed:

"To the brave Alabama boys, our opponents on this battlefield, whose memory we honor, this tablet is dedicated."

Two Great Battles

The fearful fire swept Wilderness, and the Bloody Angle at Spottsylvania

After Chancellorsville, the Confederate Army invaded the North, and Hooker left the Stafford Hills to follow Lee into Pennsylvania. When Gettysburg was over, both armies came back to face each other along the Rappahannock, twenty to thirty miles above Fredericksburg.

Now, Chancellorsville is in a quiet tract of scrub pine woods, twelve miles west of Fredericksburg. The Plank Road and the Turnpike run toward it and meet there, only to diverge three miles or so west, and six miles still further west (from Chancellorsville) the two roads cross Wilderness Run — the Turnpike crosses near Wilderness Tavern, the Plank Road about five miles southward.

Two miles from Wilderness Tavern on the Turnpike is Mine Run. Here General Meade, now commanding the Northern Army, moved his forces, and on December 1, 1863, the two armies were entrenched. But after skirmishes, Meade, who had started toward Richmond, decided not to fight and retreated with the loss of 1,000 men.

In the spring General Grant, now commander-in-chief, began to move from the vicinity of Warrenton, and on May 4, 1864, his vast army was treading the shadowed roads through the Wilderness. It was one of the greatest armies that has ever been engaged in mobile warfare; for, by official records, Grant had 141,000 men.

Lee's army — he had now 64,000 men — was moving in three columns from the general direction of Culpeper.

Grant intended to get between Lee and Richmond, but he failed, for the Confederate commander met him in the tangled Wilderness, and one of the most costly battles of the war began—a battle that can barely be touched on here, for, fought as it was in the woods, the lines wavering and shifting and the attack now from one side, now from the other, it became so involved that a volume is needed to tell the story.

It is sufficient to say that the first heavy fighting began along the Turnpike near Wilderness Run, on May 4 and 5, and that shortly afterwards the lines were heavily engaged on each side of, and parallel to, the Plank Road. Northward, on the Germanna road, charges and countercharges were made, and on May 6, Sedgwick's line finally broke and gave ground before a spirited charge by part of Ewell's corps — the brigades of Gordon, Johnston and Pegram doubling up that flank.

The Northern left (on the Plank Road), which had been driven back once, rallied on the morning of May 6, and in a counter-attack threatened disaster to the Confederates under Heth and Wilcox who (this was in the forenoon) were driven back by a terrific charge from the Federal lines near Brock Road. Expected for hours, Longstreet's march-worn men came up at this critical moment along Plank Road. Heading this column that had been moving since midnight was a brigade of Texans and toward these General Lee rode, calling:

"What troops are these?"

The first answer was simply:

"Texans, General."

"My brave Texas boys, you must charge. You *must* drive those people back," the Confederate commander said, so earnestly that the Texas troops began to form while Lee personally rallied the men who by now were pouring back from the front. Then as Longstreet's men began to go forward Lee rode with them until the line paused while the cry arose from all directions "General Lee, go to the rear. Lee to the rear." Officers seized his bridle. "If you will go to the rear, General," said an officer waving his hand toward the lines "these men will drive 'those people' back." His promise was made good,

Grants Advance Defeated

for as Lee drew back, Longstreet's men — General Longstreet himself had now reached the head of the column — rushed through the woods, driving the advancing Federals back, and piercing their lines in two places. Before a second and heavier assault the whole line fell back to entrenchments in front of Brock Road, and soon the junction of that road and Plank Road was within Longstreet's reach, and the Northern line threatened with irretrievable disaster.

And now, for the second time, just as a great victory was at hand, the Southern troops shot their leader. General Longstreet was advancing along the Plank Road with General Jenkins, at the head of the latter's troops, when — mistaken for a body of the enemy — they were fired into. General Longstreet was seriously wounded, General Jenkins killed, and the forward movement was checked for several hours, during which the Federals reinforced the defenses at the junction.

At night of May 6 Grant had been defeated of his purpose, his army driven back over a mile along a front of four miles, and terrific losses inflicted — for he lost in the Wilderness 17,666 men, while the Confederate losses were 10,641. General Hays (Federal) was killed near the junction of Plank and Brock Roads.

Fire now raged through the tangled pines and out of the smoke through the long night came the screams of the wounded, who helplessly waited the coming of the agonizing flames. Thousands of mutilated men lay there for hours and hours feeling the heated breath of that which was coming to devour them, helpless to move, while the fire swept on through the underbrush and dead leaves.

The battle had no result. Grant was badly defeated, but, unlike Burnside, Hooker and Meade, he did not retreat across the Rappahannock. Instead, pursuing his policy and figuring that 140,000 men against 60,000 men could fight until they killed the 60,000, themselves loosing two to one, and still have 20,000 left, he moved "by the flank."

The Day of "Bloody Angle"

By the morning of May 8 Grant's army, moving by the rear, was reaching Spotsylvania Court House by the Brock Road and the Chancellorsville Road. General Lee has no road to move on. But on the night of May 7 his engineers cut one through the Wilderness to Shady Grove Church and his advance guard moving over this intercepted Warren's corps two miles from the Court House and halted the advance. By the night of May 8, Lee's whole army was in a semi-circle, five or six miles in length, about the Court House. The center faced northward and crossed the Fredericksburg Road.

Grant attacked feebly on May 10, and again on May 11, and because of the lightness of these attacks Lee believed Grant would again move "by the flank" toward Richmond. But before dawn on May 12 Hancock's corps struck the apex of a salient just beyond the Court House, breaking the lines and capturing General Edward Johnson and staff and 1,200 men.

In this salient, now known as the "Bloody Angle," occurred one of the most terrible hand-to-hand conflicts of modern warfare. From dawn to dawn, in the area of some 500 acres which the deep and well-fortified trenches of the angle enclosed, more than 60,000 men fought that day. Artillery could hardly be used, because of the mixture of the lines, but nowhere in the war was such rifle fire known. The Northern forces broke the left of the salient, took part of the right, and, already having the apex, pushed their troops through. The lines swayed, advancing and retreating all day.

Toward evening the gallant Gordon advancing from base line of the Angle, with his whole command pouring in rifle fire, but mostly using the bayonet, drove back the Federals slowly, and at night the Confederates held all except the apex. But General Lee abandoned the salient after dark, and put his whole force in the base line. Here General Grant hesitated to attack him.

All along the lines about Spotsylvania desperate fighting occurred that day, but the battle was distinctly a draw. Both armies lay in their trenches, now and then skirmishing, until May 18, when Grant withdrew, again moving "by the flank," this time toward Milford, on the R., F. & P. Railroad.

Near the Bloody Angle, on the Brock Road, where it is intersected by a cross road, General Sedgwick was killed by a sharpshooter concealed in a tree. He fell from his horse, and although his aides summoned medical help he died almost immediately. The tree from which it is said the sharpshooter killed him is still standing.

General Lee had at Spotsylvania about 55,000 men and General Grant about 124,000.

The Federal loss was 15,577. The Confederate loss was 11,578. A large part of these, probably 15,000, fell in the Bloody Angle.*

(IN OTHER WARS)

In the War of 1812 only one company was formed here, commanded by Colonel Hamilton. This company did really very little service. The fear that the enemy would come up the Rappahannock River to attack this place was never realized.

In the war with Mexico it is not recorded that any distinctive company was enrolled here, although a number of its young men enlisted, and one of the Masons of Gunston was the first man killed, in the ambush of the First Dragoons on the Mexican border. General Daniel Ruggles won honor in this war.

In the Civil War, every man, "from the cradle to the grave," went to the front voluntarily and cheerfully for the cause. They could be found in such commands as the Thirtieth Virginia Regiment of Infantry, commanded by Colonel Robert S. Chew, in which, among the many officers were: Hugh S. Doggett, Robert T. Know, James S. Knox, Edgar Crutchfield, John K. Anderson, Edward Hunter, Thomas F. Proctor and many others. Of these it is sufficient to say that at all times they loyally did their duty, and this may also be said

*Figures, see official reports.

In the Great World War

of the Fredericksburg Artillery, sometimes called Braxton's Battery, among the officers of which were Carter Braxton, Edward Marye, John Pollock, John Eustace and others Some of "our boys" united themselves with the "Bloody Ninth" Virginia Cavalry, commanded by that prince of calvarimen, Colonel Thomas W. Waller, of Stafford. Others of the town, voluntarily enlisted in many other branches.

Charles T. Goolrick commanded a company of infantry which was organized and equipped by his father, Peter Goolrick. Later his health gave way and his brother, Robert Emmett Goolrick, a lieutenant in the company, took command.

When the War with Spain was declared, the old Washington Guards, which has done its duty at all times in the life of the town, came to the front. Captain Maurice B. Rowe was its commander at that time; Jas. H. Revere, first lieutenant, and Robert S. Knox, now of the U. S. Army, second lieutenant. It is pertinent to state that in the War with Spain there was no draft, and there were more volunteers than there was work to do. The company marched away with great hopes, but spent almost the whole period of the war at Camp Alger, near Washington.

When the Great World War came on, Fredericksburg sent two organized companies to the front. The first, the Washington Guards, under Captain Gunyon Harrison, and the second, the Coast Artillery Company, under Captain A. L. Johnson. No names can be recorded, for after the companies left, the draft men went in large bodies, and many won promotion and distinguished service medals.

On July 4, 1918, the town gave to the World War soldiers a sincere and royal "welcome home," in which the people testified to their gratitude to them. In the war, our boys had added luster to the name of the town, and splendid credit to themselves. The joy of the occasion and the pleasure of it were marred by the fact that so many had died in France.

Heroes of Early Days

The Old Town gives the first Commander, first Admiral, and Great Citizens

Fredericksburg claims George Washington, who although born in Westmoreland County, Virginia, February 22, 1732, spent most of his boyhood on the "Ferry Farm," the home of his father, Augustine Washington, situated on a hill directly opposite the wharf which juts out from the Fredericksburg side of the river. Here it is that Parson Weems alleged he threw a stone across the river.

He was educated in Fredericksburg and Falmouth, a village of gray mists and traditions, which lords it over Fredericksburg in the matter of quaintness and antiquity, but obligingly joins its fortunes to those of the town by a long and picturesque bridge.

His tutor in Falmouth was a "Master Hobbie," and while this domine was "strapping the unthinking end of boys," George was evading punishment by being studious and obedient. He also attended the school of Mr. Marye, at St. George's Church. It was in this church that the Washingtons worshipped.

Shy in boyhood and eclectic in the matter of associates, he had the genius for real friendships.

The cherry tree which proclaimed him a disciple of truth has still a few flourishing descendants on the old farm, and often one sees a tourist cherishing a twig as a precious souvenir of the ground hallowed by the tread of America's most famous son. It was on this farm that George was badly hurt while riding (without permission) his father's chestnut colt.

We take Washington's career almost for granted, as we watch the stars without marveling at the forces that drive them on, but when we do stop to think, we are sure to wonder at the substantial greatness, the harnessed strength of will, the sagacity and perception, which made him the man he was.

He left school at sixteen, after having mastered geometry and trigonometry, and having learned to use logarithms.

He became a surveyor. His brother, Lawrence, who at that time owned Mt. Vernon, recognized this; in fact, got him, about 1750, to survey those wild lands in the Western Frontier belonging to Lord Fairfax.

He was given a commission as public surveyor after this. It is hard to realize that he was only sixteen! We will not attempt to dwell upon his life in detail. We know that at nineteen he was given a military district, with the rank of major, in order to meet the dangers of Indian depredations and French encroachments. His salary was only 150 pounds a year.

On November 4, 1752, he was made a Mason in Fredericksburg Lodge, No. 4. The Bible used in these interesting ceremonies, is still in possession of the lodge, and is in a fine state of preservation. Washington continued a member of this lodge until he died, and Lafayette was an honorary member.

At twenty-one, as a man of "discretion, accustomed to travel, and familiar with the manners of the Indians," he was sent by Governor Dinwiddie on a delicate mission which involved encroachments by the French on property claimed by the English. During all these years he came at close intervals to visit his mother, now living in her own house in Fredericksburg, which was still his home.

After his distinguished campaign against the French army under M. De Jumonville in the region of Ohio, where he exposed himself with the most reckless bravery, he came to Mt. Vernon which he inherited from his brother, Augustus, married Martha Custis, a young widow with two children and large landed estates, and became a member of the House of Burgesses, punctually attending all the sessions.

When "George" Got Arrested

Indeed, one finds oneself eagerly looking for an occasional lapse in this epic of punctuality. It would humanize him. Anyway, one is glad to see that he was a patron of the arts and the theatre, and his industry in keeping day-books, letter-books, contracts and deeds is somewhat offset by the fact that he played the flute.

He seldom spoke in the House of Burgesses, but his opinion was eagerly sought and followed. We will pass over the time when Dunmore prorogued the "House," and of the events which ended in Washington's being made Commander-in-Chief of the Continental Army.

We are, perhaps, more interested in another visit to Fredericksburg to see his mother, after he had resigned his commission. From town and country, his friends gathered to give him welcome and do him honor. The military turned out, civic societies paraded, and cannon boomed.

In between his career as statesmen and as soldier, we strain our eyes for a thread of color, and we discover that he was once brought before a justice of the peace and fined for trading horses on Sunday. And again, that he was summoned before the grand jury and "George William Fairfax, George Washington, George Mason," and half dozen others were indicted for "not reporting their wheeled vehicles, according to law."

It is worth noting, too, that while her son, George, was leading the American army, Mary, his mother, was a partisan of the King; a tory most openly. "I am sure I shall hear some day," She told some one, calmly, in her garden, "that they have hung George."

Nevertheless, his first two messages, after he crossed the Delaware and won signal victories, were to Congress and his mother. And after the hard-riding courier had handed her the note, and the gathering people had waited until she laid down her trowel, and wiped the garden earth from her hands, she turned to them and said: "Well, George has crossed the Delaware and defeated the King's troops at Trenton."

Washington Advises Lovers

The stern fact of the Revolution, which cast upon George Washington immortal fame and which was followed by his election to the Presidency of the United States, is softened somewhat by a letter on love written to his daughter, Nellie Custis. A few excerpts are as follows:

"When the fire is beginning to kindle, and the heart growing warm, propound these questions to it. Who is this invader? Is he a man of character; a man of sense? For be assured, a sensible woman can never be happy with a fool. Is his fortune sufficient to maintain me in the manner I have been accustomed to live? And is he one to whom my friends can have no reasonable objection?"

And again, "It would be no great departure from the truth to say that it rarely happens otherwise than that a thorough paced coquette dies in celibacy, as a punishment for her attempts to mislead others by encouraging looks, words and actions, given for no other purpose than to draw men on to make overtures that they may be rejected."

The letter ends with a blessing bestowed on the young lady to whom is given such sensible advice. That this letter is characterized by an admirable poise, cannot be denied.

George Washington died at Mt. Vernon, December 14, 1799. He upheld the organization of the American state during the first eight years of its existence, amid the storms of interstate controversy, and gave it time to consolidate.

No other American but himself could have done this — for of all the American leaders he was the only one whom men felt differed from themselves. The rest were soldiers, civilians, Federalists or Democrats, but he — was Washington.

Almost immediately after appearing before the public session of Congress, at which he resigned his commission as commander-in-chief of the Continental armies, an act of which Thackeray speaks as sheathing his sword after "a life of spotless honor, a purity unreproached, a courage indomitable and a consummate victory," Washington came to Fredericks-

Evidence of Citizenship

burg to visit his mother. He was the great hero of the age, the uncrowned King of America and from all over the section crowds flocked to do him honor. The occasion was of such importance that the city did not trust the words of welcome to a single individual, but called a meeting of the City Council at which a short address was adopted and presented to Washington upon his arrival by William McWilliams, then mayor.

While beautifully worded to show the appreciation of his services and respect for his character and courage, the address of welcome contains nothing of historical significance except the line "And it affords us great joy to see you once more at a place which claims the honor of your growing infancy, the seat of your amiable parent and worthy relatives," which establishes Washington's connection with Fredericksburg.

In reply, General Washington said:

Gentlemen:

With the greatest pleasure I receive in the character of a private citizen the honor of your address. To a benevolent providence and the fortitude of a brave and virtuous army, supported by the general exertion of our common country, I stand indebted for the plaudits you now bestow. The reflection, however, of having met the congratulating smiles and approbation of my fellow citizens for the part I have acted in the cause of Liberty and Independence cannot fail of adding pleasure to the other sweets of domestic life; and my sense of them is heightened by their coming from the respectable inhabitants of the place of my growing infancy and the honorable mention which is made of my revered mother, by whose maternal hand, (early deprived of a father) I was led to manhood. For the expression of personal affection and attachment, and for your kind wishes for my future welfare, I offer grateful thanks and my sincere prayers for the happiness and prosperity of the corporate town of Fredericksburg.

Signed: GEORGE WASHINGTON.

This address is recorded in the books of the town council and is signed in a handwriting that looks like that of Washington.

As it is known that Washington lived at Fredericksburg from the time he was about six years of age until early manhood, the expression "growing infancy" is unfortunate, but later, when Mayor Robert Lewis, a nephew of Washington, delivered the welcome address to General Lafayette when he visited Fredricksburg in 1824 the real case was made more plain when he said:

"The presence of the friend of Washington excites the tenderest emotions and associations among a people whose town enjoys the distinguished honor of having been the residence of the Father of his Country during the days of his childhood and youth," and in reply General Lafayette said:

"At this place, Sir, which calls to our recollections several among the most honored names of the Revolutionary War, I did, many years ago, salute the first residence of our paternal chief, receiving the blessings of his venerated mother and of his dear sister, your own respected mother." Later the same day, at a banquet in the evening, given in his honor, Lafayette offered the following sentiment, "The City of Fredericksburg — first residence of Washington — may she more and more attain all the prosperity which independence, republicanism and industry cannot fail to secure."

JOHN PAUL JONES.

Of all the men whose homes were in Fredericksburg, none went forth to greater honor nor greater ignominy than John Paul Jones, who raised the first American flag on the masthead of his ship, died in Paris and was buried and slept for 113 years beneath a filthy stable yard, forgotten by the country he valiantly served.

He came to Fredericksburg early in 1760 on "The Friendship," as a boy of thirteen years. Born in a lowly home, he was a mere apprentice seaman, and without doubt he deserted his ship in those days, when sea life was a horror, to come to Fredericksburg and join his brother, William Paul, whose home was here, and who is buried here. There is some record of his having been befriended by a man in Carolina, and traditions that he left his ship in a port on the Rappahannock after killing a sailor, and walked through the wilderness to Fredericksburg. Neither tradition is of importance; the fact is that he came here and remained four years during the developing period of his life.

William Paul had immigrated to Fredericksburg from the Parish of Kirkbeam, Scotland, (where he and his brother,

Jones' American House Here

John, were born), about 1760, had come to Fredericksburg and conducted a grocery store and tailor shop on the corner of Caroline and Prussia streets. William died here in 1773, and is buried in St. George's Church Yard. In his will he left his property to sisters in the Parish of Kirkbeam, Scotland.

Alexander McKenzie, in his life of John Paul Jones, says, after referring to the fact that William Paul is buried in Fredericksburg: "In 1773 he went back to Fredericksburg to arrange the affairs of his brother, William Paul," and John Paul Jones himself wrote of Fredericksburg: "It was the home of my fond election since first I saw it." The Legislature of Virginia decided in settling William Paul's estate that John Paul Jones was a legal resident of Fredericksburg.

Obviously, then, Fredericksburg was the great Admiral's home, for, though not born here, he chose it when he came to America.

When he first reached the little town on the Rappahannock he went to work for his brother, William Paul and one can surmise that he clerked and carried groceries and messages to the gentry regarding their smart clothes for his brother.

The Rising Sun Tavern was then a gathering place for the gentry and without doubt he saw them there. He may well have learned good manners from their ways, good language from hearing their conversation and "sedition" from the great who gathered there. We may picture the lowly boy, lingering in the background while the gentlemen talked and drank punch around Mine Host Weedon's great fire, or listening eagerly at the counter where the tavern-keeper, who was to be a Major-General, delivered the mail.

Certainly John Paul Jones was a lowly and uneducated boy at 13. He left Fredericksburg after four years to go to sea again, and in 1773 came back to settle his brother's estate, and remained here until December 22, 1775, when he received at Fredericksburg his commission in the Navy.

John Paul Jones' story is more like romance than history. Beginning an uncouth lad, he became a sea fighter whose

From Cabin Boy to Courtier

temerity outranks all. We see him aboard the Bonhomme Richard, a poor thing for seafaring, fighting the Serapis just off British shores, half of his motley crew of French and Americans dying or dead about him, the scruppers running blood, mad carnage raging, and when he is asked if he is ready to surrender he says: "I've just begun to fight," and by his will forcing victory out of defeat. He was the only American who fought the English on English soil. He never walked a decent quarter deck, but with the feeble instruments he had, he captured sixty superior vessels. His ideal of manliness was courage.

What of this Fredericksburg gave him no one may say, but it is sure that the chivalry, grace and courtliness which admitted him in later years to almost every court in Europe was absorbed from the gentry in Virginia. He did not learn it on merchantmen or in his humble Scotch home, and so he learned it here. Of him the Duchess de Chartres wrote:

"Not Bayard, nor Charles le Téméaire could have laid his helmet at a lady's feet with such knightly grace."

He won his country's high acclaim, but it gave him no substantial evidence. He was an Admiral in the Russian Navy, and after a time he went to Paris to live a few years in poverty, neglect, and bitterness. He died and was buried in Paris in 1792, at 45 years of age.

He was a dandy, this John Paul Jones, who walked the streets of Fredericksburg in rich dress. Lafayette, Jefferson, and, closest of all, the Scotch physician, Hugh Mercer, were his friends. Slender and not tall, black-eyed and swarthy, with sensitive eyes, and perfect mouth and chin, he won the love or friendship of women quicker than that of men.

He was buried in an old graveyard in Paris and forgotten until the author of this book wrote for newspapers a series of letters about him. Interest awoke and Ambassador Porter was directed to search for his body. How utterly into oblivion had slipped the youth who ventured far, and conquered always, is plain when it is known that it took the Ambassador six years to find the body of Commodore John Paul Jones. He found it in an old cemetery where bodies were heaped three deep under the courtyard of a stable and a laundry.

Official proof that Jones was a "citizen of Virginia" and lived in Fredericksburg is found easily in Virginia Records, and his official (U. S.) history.

Surgeon Laurens Brooke

Surgeon Laurens Brooke, was born in Fredericksburg, in 1720, and was one of those who accompanied Governor Spottswood as a Knight of the Golden Horseshoe. He afterwards lived in Fredericksburg, entered the U. S. Navy as a surgeon and sailed with John Paul Jones on the "Ranger" and on the "Bon Homme Richard." At the famous battle of Scarborough, between the latter vessel and the "Serapis," Surgeon Brooke alone had the care of one hundred and twenty wounded sailors; and later with Surgeon Edgerly, of the English navy, from the Tempis, performed valiant work and saved many lives. The surgeons were honored by Captain Paul Jones with a place at his mess, and the literature of the period refers to Surgeon Brooke as the "good old Doctor Laurens Brooke." He was with Jones until the end of the war and spent some time at his home here when a very old man, some years after the Revolution. His family had a distinguished part in the War Between the States, being represented in the army and in the C. S. Congress during that period.

General Hugh Mercer

We wonder if any one ever declined to take the advice of George Washington.

Certain it is that General Hugh Mercer did not, for, at the suggestion of Washington, Mercer came to Fredericksburg. Many Scotchmen have found the town to their liking. It makes them feel a sort of kinship with the country of hill-shadows, and strange romance.

Major General Hugh Mercer

Mercer was born in Aberdeen in the year 1725. His father was a clergyman; his mother, a daughter of Sir Robert Munro, who, after distinguishing himself at Fontenoy and elsewhere, was killed at the battle of Falkirk, while opposing the young "Pretender." Hugh Mercer did not follow in the footsteps of his father, but linked his fortunes with Charles Edward's army, as assistant surgeon, fought with him at Culloden and shared the gloom of his defeat — a defeat which was not less bitter because his ears were ringing with the victorious shouts of the army of the Duke of Cumberland.

To change a scene that brought sad memories, Dr. Hugh Mercer, in the fall of 1746, embarked for America. There, on the frontiers of civilization, in Western Pennsylvania, he spent arduous, unselfish years. He was welcomed and loved in this unsettled region of scattered homes.

A rough school it was in which the doctor learned the lessons of life.

In the year 1755, Mercer made his appearance in the ill-fated army of Braddock, which met humiliating disaster at Fort Duquesne. Washington's splendid career began here and here Mercer was wounded. Of this memorable day of July 9, 1755, it has been said that "The Continentals gave the only glory to that humiliating disaster."

In 1756, while an officer in a military association, which was founded to resist the aggression of the French and Indians, he was wounded and forced to undergo terrible privations. While pursued by savage foes he sought refuge in the trunk of a tree, around which the Indians gathered and discussed the prospect of scalping him in the near future. When they left he escaped in the opposite direction and completely outwitted them. Then began a lonely march through an unbroken forest, where he was compelled to live on roots and herbs, and where the carcass of a rattlesnake proved his most nourishing meal. He finally succeeded in rejoining his command at Fort Cumberland. In recognition of

Mercer Joins Masonic Lodge

his sacrifices and services in these Indian wars, the Corporation of Philadelphia presented him with a note of thanks and a splendid memorial medal. In the year 1758 he met George Washington and then it was that Pennsylvania lost a citizen. In Fredericksburg, at the time that Mercer came, lived John Paul Jones, and we do not doubt that they often met and talked of their beloved Scotland.

During his first years in Fredericksburg, Mercer occupied a small two-story house on the southwest corner of Princess Anne and Amelia Streets. There he had his office and apothecary shop. The building is still standing.

An Englishman, writing at this time of a visit to Fredericksburg, calls Mercer "a man of great eminence and possessed of almost every virtue and accomplishment," truly a sweeping appreciation.

He belonged to Lodge No. 4, of which George Washington was also a member, and he occasionally paid a visit to Mount Vernon.

In September, 1774, the Continental Congress met in Philadelphia. The war cloud was lowering, it broke, and when the Revolution swept the country, Mercer was elected Colonel of the Third Virginia Regiment.

An approbation of the choice of Mercer was prepared by the county committee, which set forth the importance of the appointment and was an acknowledgment of his public spirit and willingness to sacrifice his life.

Colonel Mercer with his men and fifes and drums marched away from his home, bidding good-bye to his wife (Isabella Gordon), whom he never saw again.

There is an interesting story of Mercer at Williamsburg. Among the troops which were sent there at that time, was a Company of riflemen from beyond the mountains, commanded by a Captain Gibson. A reckless and violent opposition to military restraint had gained for this corps the

Mercer Quells a Mutiny

name of "Gibson's Lambs." After a short time in camp, a mutiny arose among them, causing much excitement in the army, and alarming the inhabitants of the city. Free from all restraint, they roamed through the camp, threatening with instant death any officer who would presume to exercise any authority over them.

At the height of the mutiny an officer was dispatched with the alarming tidings to the quarters of Colonel Mercer. The citizens of the town vainly implored him not to risk his life in this infuriated mob.

Reckless of personal safety, he instantly repaired to the barracks of the mutinous band and directing a general parade of the troops, he ordered Gibson's company to be drawn up as offenders and violators of the law, and to be disarmed in his presence.

The ringleaders were placed under a strong guard and in the presence of the whole army he addressed the offenders in an eloquent manner, impressing on them their duties as citizens and soldiers, and the certainty of death if they continued to remain in that mutinous spirit equally disgraceful to them and hazardous to the sacred interests they had marched to defend. Disorder was instantly checked and the whole company was ever afterward as efficient in deportment as any troop in the army.

On June 5, 1776, Mercer was made Brigadier-General in the Continental Army. It was Mercer who suggested to Washington the crossing of the Delaware. Major Armstrong, Mercer's Aide-de-Camp, who was present at a council of officers, and who was with Mercer on that fateful night, is authority for this statement.

We, somehow, see the army of the colonists poorly clad, many of them barefoot, without tents, with few blankets, and badly fed. In front of them is Cornwallis, with his glittering hosts, and we can almost hear the boast of General Howe, that Philadelphia would fall when the Delaware froze. He

Death on The Battlefield

did not know Washington; and Mercer's daring was not reckoned with. We wonder if ever a Christmas night was so filled with history as that on which Washington, with the intrepid Mercer at his side, pushing through that blinding storm of snow and fighting his way through the floating ice, crossed the Deleware with the rallying cry of "victory or death," and executed the brilliant move which won for him the Battle of Trenton.

Near Princeton, Washington's army was hemmed in by Cornwallis in front and the Delaware in the rear. After a consultation at Mercer's headquarters it was determined to withdraw the Continental forces from the front of the enemy near Trenton, and attack the detachment then at Princeton. The pickets of the two armies were within two hundred yards of each other. In order to deceive the enemy, campfires were left burning on Washington's front line and thus deceived, the enemy slept.

A woman guided the Continental army on that night march. A detachment of two hundred men, under Mercer, was sent to seize a bridge at Worth's Mill. The night had been dreary; the morning was severely cold. Mercer's presence was revealed at daybreak. General Mahood counter-marched his regiment and crossed the bridge at Worth's Mill before Mercer could reach it. The British troops charged. The Colonials were driven back. General Mercer dismounted and tried vainly to rally his men. While he was doing this, he was attacked by a group of British troops, who, with the butts of muskets, beat him down and demanded that he surrender. He refused. He was then bayoneted and left for dead on the battlefield. Stabbed in seven different places, he did not expire until January 12, 1777.

Washington finally won the Battle of Princeton, but Mercer was a part of the price he paid. The battles of Trenton and Princeton were the most brilliant victories in the War of the Revolution.

Sir Lewis Littlepage

At Fredericksburg a monument perpetuates Mercer's fame. At the funeral in Philadelphia 30,000 people were present, and there his remains rest in Laurel Hill Cemetery.

The St. Andrew's Society, which he joined in 1757, erected a monument to his memory and in the historical painting of the Battle of Princeton, by Peale Mercer is given a prominent place. The states of Pennsylvania, Kentucky, Virginia and New Jersey have, by an act of Legislature, named a county "Mercer," and on October 1, 1897, a bronze tablet to his memory was unveiled at Princeton, N. J. We have not the space to relate all of his illustrious life, but somewhere there is a poem, the last lines of which voice the sentiment of his countrymen.

> "But he, himself, is canonized,
> If saintly deeds such fame can give;
> As long as liberty is prized,
> Hugh Mercer's name shall surely live."

Sir Lewis Littlepage

In the possession of a well-known man of Richmond, Va., is a large gold key.

It is vastly different from the keys one sees these days, and inquiry develops that it was once the property of one of the most picturesque characters in America — a man who began his life in the cornfields of Hanover County, Va., in 1753, and was swept by the wave of circumstance into the palace of a King.

The atmosphere of old William and Mary College, where Lewis Littlepage was graduated, after the death of his father, gave a mysteriously romantic note to the beckoning song of adventure, which finally became a definite urge, when the youth, after residing in Fredericksburg, listened to the advice of his guardian, Benjamin Lewis, of Spotsylvania County, who placed him with John Jay, the American Minister at Madrid.

The Poet Takes a Sword

Six months later, Jay, in a letter to Benjamin Lewis, said of the seveteen-year-old lad:

"I am much pleased with your nephew, Lewis Littlepage, whom I regard as a man of undoubted genius, and a person of unusual culture."

And a few months after this we discover that the well-known traveler, Mr. Elekiah Watson, has an entry in his diary which reads:

"At Nantes I became acquainted with Lewis Littlepage, and although he is but eighteen years of age, I believe him to be the most remarkable character of the age. I esteem him a prodigy of genius."

In Madrid, Littlepage got into financial straits, owing to the fact that his allowance did not reach him, and the next glimpse we get of him is through the smoke of battle at Fort Mahon, where in 1781, as a member of the force under the Duke de Crillion, he was painfully wounded while charging the Turks.

In 1872, en route to Madrid to join Mr. Jay, he heard that de Crillion was preparing to storm Gibraltar, and, believing himself in honor bound to follow the fortunes of his chief, he wrote Mr. Jay that he must turn again to arms.

From that day forward he was a soldier, a diplomat, a courtier — the elected friend of Kings and Princes.

He aided in storming Gibraltar and left his ship only when it had burned to the water's edge. He was highly recommended to the King for his gallantry, and went back to Paris with de Crillion to become a brilliant figure at court and in the salons.

Europe knew him, but America refused him even a small commission, though Kings wrote to our Congress in his behalf.

He met Lafayette at Gibraltar; in fact, accompanied him to Spain. Then, after considerable travel in European countries, he again encountered Prince Nassau, who was his brother at arms in de Crillion's forces, became his aide-de-camp and, together they found happiness in travel. They sought the bright lights of gay capitals and followed mysterious moon tracks on the Danube river.

At the Diet of Grodno, in 1784, where he went with Nassau, he met Stanislaus Augustus, King of Poland. He captivated the King; and in a brilliant ball room, Stansilaus offered him a permanent service at his court.

Within a year he was chamberlain and secretary to the cabinet of His Majesty, and for years he was practically the ruler of the empire.

In 1787, at Kiva, he made a treaty with Catherine, Empress of Russia, and became her intimate friend.

He was a special and secret envoy from Poland to the sessions of the grand quadruple alliance in France. Later we see him leading a division of the army of Prince Potempkin across the snow-clad steppes of Russia, and a few months after, he was marching at the head of the Prince's army through the wild reaches of Tartary. Again, under Prince Nassau, we find him commanding a fleet against the Turks at Oczacon.

Shortly after, he was a special high commissioner to Madrid. His mission completed, he was ordered to return to Russia for the revolution of 1791, and now he served as aide-de-camp and Major-General.

In 1794, when the Polish patriot, Kosciusco, headed a revolution, Littlepage answered his summons and fought through to the storming of Prague.

Stanislaus held him the greatest of his generals and his aides and when the King was captured by the Russians, Littlepage, tired of the broils of European politics, came home to America.

When Littlepage was first in Poland, the place was gay and laughter-loving. An atmosphere of high culture and literary achievements made a satisfactory entourage for the ill-North Poland. There were starlight meetings and woodland fated people. He lived happily there and loved a princess of

Ah, But he Had His Memories

strolls, vows of faith and the pain of renunciation, when for diplomatic reasons she was forced to endure another alliance. Littlepage's reputation and splendid appearance; her beauty and the love they bore each other and, finally, her death, made a background of red romance, against which he is silhouetted in one's memory.

That Lewis Littlepage was a poet of no mean ability was a fact too well known to be disputed. The last verse of a poem written by him and inspired by the death of the woman he loved reads:

"Over there, where you bide — past the sunset's gold glory,
   With eyes that are shining, and red lips apart,
Are you waiting to tell me the wonderful story,
   That death cannot part us — White Rose of my Heart."

It is said that Littlepage had more honors and decorations showered upon him than any other American in history.

Go to the old Masonic cemetery in Fredericksburg, and in a far corner, where the wild vines and the hardy grass struggle for mastery, you may see a legend inscribed upon a large flat stone: this is the tomb of Lewis Littlepage. For the multitude, it is simply an unpleasant finale to the life of a well known man.

To the imaginative, it starts a train of thought — a play of fancy. One sees the rise of the star of Poland. Gay youths and maids pass and repass to the sound of music and laughter. The clank of a sword sounds above the measured foot fall on a polished floor. A soldier passes in all the bravery of uniform. It is General Littlepage silently going to an audience with the King. The massive doors open without a challenge, for as a passport to the palace, on the uniform of this soldier glitters a large gold key — the gift of Stanislaus.

Suddenly the scene changes. Amid the surging hosts and in the thick of the bloody clash at Prague, when the anguish of uncertainty was crumbling the courage of a kingdom, a man is seen, riding with reckless abandon. Tearing through the lines and holding aloft the tattered standard of Poland, comes Littlepage of Virginia. With the rallying cry of his adopted land, he gathers up his troops and gloriously defends the flag he loves. Our eyes again stray to the legend on the tomb: Disillusionment!

His return to his old home! His death! We see this also, but with this is the knowledge that he lived greatly, and in his ears, while dying, sounded again the shout of victory, while his heart held the dream of the old romance.

Gen. George Weedon

Among the first men in America to "fan the flames of sedition," as an English traveler said of him long before the war, was Mine Host George Weedon, keeper of the Rising Sun Tavern, Postmaster, and an Irish immigrant. At his place gathered all the great of his day, spending hours dicing and drinking punch.

Over and over among these men — Washington, Mason, Henry, the Lees, Jefferson and every Virginia gentleman of that section, George Weedon heard discussion of the Colonies' problems, and he forcibly gave vent to his opinions.

Time and again he expressed the idea of freedom before others had thought of more than protest. His wild Irish talk in the old Rising Sun Tavern helped to light the torch of liberty in America.

When war came, Weedon was elected Lieutenant-Colonel of the First Virginia, of which Hugh Mercer was chosen Colonel. August 17, 1776, he became its Colonel, and on February 24, 1777, he was made a Brigadier-General.

In the Battle of Brandywine, General Weedon's division rendered conspicuous service, when they checked the pursuit of the British and saved our army from rout. He commanded brilliantly at Germantown. Wherever he fought, his great figure and stentorian voice were prominent in the conflict.

A Song For The Yuletide

He admired Washington and his fellow-generals. It was not because of these, but because he thought Congress to have treated him unfairly about rank, that he left the Army at Valley Forge. He re-entered in 1780, and in 1781 was given command of the Virginia troops, which he held until the surrender of Yorktown, where he played an important part.

George Weedon was the first President of the Virginia Society of the Cincinnati, a fraternity of Revolutionary officers which General Washington helped to organize, and this was, indeed, a singular honor. He was a member of the Fredericksburg Masonic Lodge, of which Washington was also a member. After the war, he lived at "The Sentry Box," the former home of his gallant brother-in-law, General Mercer.

General Weedon was a man of exuberant spirits, loud of voice and full of Irish humor. He wrote a song called "Christmas Day in '76," and on each Yuletide he assembled at his board his old comrades and friends, and, while two negro boys stood sentinel at the door, drank punch and roared out the verses:

> "On Christmas Day in '76
> Our ragged troops with bayonets fixed,
>   For Trenton marched away.
> The Delaware ice, the boats below
> The lights obscured by hail and snow,
>   But no signs of dismay."

Beginning thus, the brave Irishman who verbally and physically fought among the foremost for America for over thirty years, told the story of Washington's crossing the Delaware, vividly enough, and every Christmas his guests stood with him and sang the ballad.*

---
*See Goolrick's "Life of Mercer."

Mason of Gunston

Of George Mason, whom Gaillard Hunt says is "more than any other man entitled to be called the Father of the Declaration of Independence," whom Judge Harlan says, "Is the greatest political philosopher the Western Hemisphere ever produced," of whose Bill of Rights, Gladstone said "It is the greatest document that ever emanated from the brain of man," little can be said here. His home was at Gunston Hall, on the Potomac, but the Rising Sun knew him well, and his feet often trod Mary Washington's garden walks, or the floors of Kenmore, Chatham and the other residences of Old Fredericksburg.

Mason was intimate here, and here much of his trading and shipping was done. When he left Gunston, it was usually to come to Fredericksburg and meet his younger conferees, who were looking up to him as the greatest leader in America. He died and is buried at Gunston Hall. It was in Fredericksburg that he first met young Washington, who ever afterward looked upon "The Sage of Gunston" as his adviser and friend, and as America's greatest man.

General William Woodford

Although he came from Caroline, General William Woodford was a frequenter of and often resident in Fredericksburg, and it was from this city he went to Caroline upon the assembling of troops when Lord Dunmore became hostile. In subsequent military operations he was made Colonel of the Second Regiment and distinguished himself in the campaign that followed, and he was honorably mentioned for his valiant conduct at the battle of Gread Bridge, December 9, 1775, upon which occasion he had the chief command and gained a brilliant victory. He was later made General of the First Virginia Brigade. His command was in various actions throughout the war, in one of which, the Battle of Brandywine, he was severely wounded. He was made prisoner by the British in 1778 at Charleston, and taken to New York, where he died.

The Owner of "Kenmore"

Col. Fielding Lewis

The mansion stands in a park, which in autumn is an explosion of color. An old wall, covered with Virginia creeper, adds a touch of glamour to the Colonial house, and a willow tree commanding a conspicuous corner of the grounds lends a melancholy aspect which makes up the interesting atmosphere of Kenmore, part of the estate of Colonel Fielding Lewis, who brought to this home his bride, "Betty," a sister of George Washington, and where they lived as befitted people of wealth and learning, his wife giving an added meaning to the social life of the old town, and Colonel Lewis himself taking an active and prominent part in the civic affairs, as most people of wealth and culture deemed it their duty to do in the days gone by.

Colonel Lewis was an officer in the Patriot Army and commanded a division at the siege of Yorktown. He was an ardent patriot and when the Revolution started his activities ran to the manufacture of firearms, which were made at "The Gunnery" from iron wrought at the foundry, traces of which may still be seen on the Rappahannock river, just above the village of Falmouth.

Colonel Lewis was a magistrate in the town after the war, a member of the City Council and represented the county in the Legislature.

His son, Captain Robert Lewis, was one of President Washington's private secretaries and mayor of Fredericksburg from 1821 to the day of his death. When LaFayette visited the town in 1824, Colonel Lewis was selected to deliver the address of welcome.

However, we are apt to forget the elegancies and excellencies of the courtly man whose life was dedicated to useful service in a note that is struck by the home in which he lived. Kenmore, in the light of its past, sounds an overtone of romance. We cannot escape it, and it persistently reverberates above the people it sheltered. Kenmore was built in 1750.

The Greatest Officeholder

JAMES MONROE

James Monroe was among the most important citizens that ever lived in Fredericksburg.

Monroe was born in Westmoreland County, not far from what is now Colonial Beach. When a young man he was attracted by the larger opportunities afforded by the town and moved to Fredericksburg, where he began the practice of law, having an office in the row of old brick buildings on the west side of Charles Street, just south of Commerce. Records still in the courthouse show that he bought property on lower Princess Anne Street, which still is preserved and known as "The Home of James Monroe." Monroe occupied the house when it was located at Bradley's corner, and it was afterwards moved to its present site, though some contend that he lived in the house on its present site.

Shortly after his arrival he became affiliated with St. George's Church, soon being elected a vestryman, and when he had been here the proper length of time he got into politics, and was chosen as one of the Town Councilmen. From this humble political preferment at the hands of the Fredericksburg people, he began a career that seemed ever afterward to have included nothing but officeholding. Later he became Continental Congressman from the district including Fredericksburg, and was, in turn, from that time on, Representative in the Virginia convention, Governor of Virginia, United States Congressman, Envoy Extraordinary to France, again Governor, Minister to England, Secretary of War, once more Minister to England, Minister to Madrid, Secretary of State and twice President — if not a world's record at least one that is not often overmatched. Previous to his political career, Monroe had served in the Revolutionary Army as a Captain, having been commissioned while a resident of Fredericksburg.

Monroe gave to America one of its greatest documents — known to history as the Monroe Doctrine. It was directed essentially against the purposes of the Holy Alliance, formed in 1815 by the principal European powers with the fundamental object of putting down democratic movements on the part of the people, whether they arose abroad or on this side of the world. After consultation with English statesmen and with Jefferson, Adams, John Quincy Adams and Calhoun, Monroe announced his new principle which declared that the United States of America would resent any attempt of the Alliance to "extend their system to this part of the Hemisphere."

Dr. Charles Mortimer

In a beautiful old home on lower Main Street, surrounded by a wall, mellowed by time, and ivy-crowned, lived Washington's dear friend and physician, Dr. Charles Mortimer. He could often be seen, in the days gone by, seated on his comfortable "verandah," smoking a long pipe, covered with curious devices, and discussing the affairs of the moment with those rare intellects who were drawn there by the interesting atmosphere of blended beauty and mentality. There was, as a background, a garden, sloping to the river, and sturdy trees checquered the sunlight. Old-fashioned flowers nodded in the breeze which blew up from the Rappahannock, and the Doctor's own tobacco ships, with their returned English cargoes, swung on their anchors at the foot of the terraces.

If one entered the house at the dinner hour, every delicacy of land and water would conspire against a refusal to dine with the host of this hospitable mansion. Highly polished and massive pewter dishes, disputed possession of the long mahogany table, with a mammoth bowl of roses—arrogantly secure of an advantageous position in the center.

There was often the sound of revelry by night, and the rafters echoed gay laughter and the music of violins — high, and sweet and clear.

An historic dinner, following the famous Peace Ball at the old Market House in November, 1784, was given here, and the hostess, little Maria Mortimer, sixteen years old, the

Doctor's only daughter, with her hair "cruped high" for the first time, presided, and her bon mots won the applause of the company, which was quite a social triumph for a sixteen-year-old girl, trying to hold her own with Lafayette, Count d'Estang and the famous Rochambeau. They clicked glasses and drank to her health standing, and little Maria danced with "Betty Lewis' Uncle George himself," for Washington did not disdain the stately measures of the minuet.

But there is an obverse here. The old Doctor did not fail in his duty. On horseback, with his saddlebag loaded with medicines, he rode down dark forest paths to the homes of pioneers, traveled the streets of Fredericksburg and came silently along lone trails in the country in the dead of night, when hail or snow or driving rains cut at him bitterly through the trees. He refused no call, and claimed small fees. He was Mary Washington's physician for years, called on her almost daily, and stood by her bedside mute, when, the struggle over, she quietly passed on to the God in whom she had put her deepest faith.

Of the many people who walk in Hurkamp Park, in the center of the old town, there are few who know that they are passing daily over the grave of the genial and popular Doctor, who was Fredericksburg's first mayor, and Washington's dearest friend.

MATTHEW FONTAINE MAURY

Of all the famous men who went from Fredericksburg to take large parts in the rapidly moving history of America, or in the work of the world, Commodore Maury added most to the progress of science. Not only did he create knowledge, but he created wealth by the immense saving he effected to shipping by charting shorter ocean routes. He is buried in Hollywood Cemetery, in Richmond, under a simple shaft which bears the name, "Matthew Fontaine Maury." The great "pathfinder of the seas" was born in Spotsylvania County, January, 1806, and died at Lexington in 1873.

A World Famed Scientist

He wore the most prized decorations the monarchs of Europe could give him; he founded the most valuable natural science known, and was reckoned a transcendent genius. Of him, Mellin Chamberlain, Librarian of Congress, said, with calm consideration "I do not suppose there is the least doubt that Maury was the greatest man America ever produced."

Alexander Humbolt said that Maury created a new science.

He plunged into the unknown; he charted the seas and mapped its currents and winds. He was the first to tell the world that winds and currents were not of chance, but of fixed and immutable laws, and that even cyclones were well governed. He knew why a certain coast was dry and another rainy, and he could, on being informed of the latitude and longitude of a place, tell what was the prevailing weather and winds.

Maury went to sea as a midshipman in the American navy in 1825, and in 1831, at twenty-four years of age, he became master of the sloop Falmouth, with orders to go to the Pacific waters, but, though he sought diligently, he found no chart of a track for his vessel, no record of currents or of winds to guide him. The sea was a trackless wilderness, and the winds were things of vagrant caprice. And he began then to grapple with those problems which were to immortalize him.

He came back from ocean wanderings in a few years and married an old sweetheart, Miss Ann Herndon, of Fredericksburg, and he lived for a time on Charlotte Street, between Princess Anne and Prince Edward, and wrote his first book, "A Treatise on Navigation;" while from his pen came a series of newspaper and magazine articles that startled the world of scientific thought. For the man had discovered new and unsuspected natural laws!

Misfortune — that vastly helped him — came in 1839, when his leg was injured through the overturning of a stage coach. The government put him in charge of a new "Bureau of Charts and Instruments," at Washington, and out of his work here grew the Naval Observatory, the Signal Service and the first Weather Bureau ever established on earth! Every other science was old. His science was utterly new, a field untouched.

He found a mass of log books of American warships. Over these he pondered. He sent hundreds of bottles and buoys to be dropped into the seven seas by fighting craft and merchantmen.

These were picked up now and again and came back to him, and from the information sent to him with them, and soundings in thousands of places, added to what he had gleaned in earlier years, he prepared his greatest work. It took ultimate form in a series of six "charts" and eight large volumes of "sailing directions," that comprehended all the waters and winds in all climes, and on every sea where white sails bend and steamer smoke drifts.

The charts exhibit, with wonderful accuracy, the winds and currents, their force and direction at different seasons, the calm belts, the trade winds, the rains and storms—the gulf stream, the Japan current—all the great ocean movements; and the sailing directions are treasure chests for seamen. Paths were marked out on the ocean, and a practical result was, that one of the most difficult sea voyages —from New York to San Francisco, around the Horn — was shortened by forty days. It has been estimated that by shortening the time of many sea voyages, Commander Maury has effected a saving of not less than $40,000,000 each year.

Of his own work, Maury wrote:

"So to shape the course on voyages at sea as to make the most of winds and currents, is the perfection of the navigator's art. How the winds blow or the currents flow along this route or that is no longer a matter of speculation or opinion. The wind and weather, daily encountered by hundreds who sailed before him, have been tabulated for the mariner; nay, the path has been blazed for him on the sea; mile posts have been set upon the waves and time tables furnished for the trackless waste."

It was this work that, reaching over Europe and Asia, brought on the Brussels conference in 1853, to which Maury, founder of the science of hydrography and meteorology, went as America's representative, and here he covered himself with honors. He came back to write his "Physical Geography of the Sea and Its Meteorology."

This, the essence of his life work, the poetry and the romance of his science, passed through twenty editions and was known in every school, but the book's greatest interest was killed by the removal of the poetic strain that made it beautiful. It has been translated into almost every language. In it is the story of the sea, its tides and winds, its shore lines and its myriads of life; its deep and barren bottoms. For Maury also charted the ocean floors, and it was his work in this line that caused Cyrus Field to say of the laying of the Atlantic cable:

"Maury furnished the brains, England furnished the money, and I did the work."

No other American ever was honored by Emperors and Kings as was Matthew Fontaine Maury. He was given orders of Knighthood by the Czar of Russia, the King of Denmark, King of Spain, King of Portugal, King of Belgium and Emperor of France, while Russia, Austria, Sweden, Holland, Sardenia, Bremen, Turkey and France struck gold medals in his honor. The pope of Rome sent him a full set of all the medals struck during his pontificate. Maximilian decorated him with "The Cross of the Order of Guadaloupe" while Germany bestowed on him the "Cosmos Medal," struck in honor of Von Humboldt, and the only duplicate of that medal in existence.

The current of the Civil War swept Maury away from Washington, and he declined offers from France, Germany and Russia, joining his native state in the Confederacy. He introduced the submarine torpedo, and rendered the South other service before the final wreck, which left him stranded and penniless. He went to Mexico now, to join his fortunes with those of the unhappy Maximilian, and when the Emperor met his tragic end he found himself again resourceless — and crippled. In 1868 when general amnesty was given, he came back to become the first professor of meteorology at the Virginia Military Institute. In October, 1872, he became ill and died in February of the next year.

And this man, who had from Kings and Emperors more decorations than any American has ever received, and for whom Europe had ever ready the highest honors and greatest praise, was ignored by his own government, to which he gave his life's work. No word of thanks, no tribute of esteem, no reward, was ever given him. A bill to erect a monument to him lies now rotting in some pigeonhole in Congress. But an effort to renew this is underway.

Archibald McPherson

Curiously enough, no more memory is left to Fredericksburg of Archibald McPherson than the tombstone under the mock orange tree in St. George's Church, the tablets to his memory in the old charity school on Hanover Street (now the Christian Science Church) and a few shadowy legends and unmeaning dates.

He was born in Scotland and died in Fredericksburg in 1854. He was a member of St. George's Church and vestry.

But what manner of man he was, the few recorded acts we know will convey to every one. He established a Male Charity School with his own funds principally, and took a deep interest in it, and, dying, he left the small fortune he had accumulated by Scotch thrift "to the poor of the town," and provided means of dispensing the interest on this sum for charity throughout the years to come. Most of this fund was wiped out by depreciation of money, etc., during the Civil War.

Men of Modern Times

Soldiers, Adventurers and Sailors, Heroes and Artists, mingle here.

A prophet without honor in his own country was Moncure Daniel Conway because, a Fredericksburger and a Southerner, he opposed slavery. But his genius won him world praise, and later, honor in his own country.

Born in 1832, near Falmouth, to which village his people moved later, the child of Walker Peyton Conway and Marguerite Daniel Conway he inherited from a long line of ancestry, a brilliant intellect and fearlessness to tread the paths of freedom.

The difficult studious child was too much for his teacher, Miss Gaskins, of Falmouth, so he was sent, at the age of ten, to Fredericksburg Classical and Mathematical Academy, originally John Marye's famous school, and made rapid progress.

His hero was his great uncle, Judge R. C. L. Moncure, of Glencairne, and his early memoirs are full of loving gratitude for the great man's toleration and help. The Methodism of his parents did not hold him, for he several times attended the services at St. George's Church.

The wrongs of slavery he saw, and after he entered Dickinson College, at Carlisle, in his fifteenth year, he found an anti-slavery professor, McClintock, who influenced him and encouraged his dawning agnosticism. His cousin, John M. Daniel, editor of the Richmond Examiner, became, in 1848, a leading factor in Conway's life, encouraging his literary efforts and publishing many of his contributions.

All beauty, all art appealed to him. Music was always a passion, and we also find constant and quaint references to beautiful women and girls. It seemed the superlative compliment, though he valued feminine brains and ability.

His great spiritual awakening came with his finding an article by Emerson and at the age of twenty, to the delight of his family, he became a Methodist minister.

His career as such was not a success. After one of his sermons, in which he ignored Heaven and Hell, his father said: "One thing is certain, Monk, should the Devil aim at a Methodist preacher, you'd be safe."

He moved to Cambridge. The prominence of his Southern family, and his own social and intellectual charms gave him entre to the best homes and chiefest among them, that of his adored Emerson, where he met and knew all the great lights of the day. His slavery opinions, valuable as a Southern slave owner's son, made him an asset in the anti-slavery propaganda of the time.

Among his friends were the Thoreaus, Hawthorne, Longfellow, Oliver Wendell Holmes and Agassiz.

One must hurry over the charm of those college days to Moncure Conway's first Unitarian Church, in Washington. So pronounced were his sermons on anti-slavery that his father advised him not to come home on a visit. He did come and had the humiliation of being ordered from Falmouth under pain of tar and feathers, an indignity which cut him to his soul. His success in Washington was brilliant, but he found trouble, owing to his abolitionist opinions, and had to resign. In 1856 he accepted a call to a Cincinnati church, whose literary and artistic circles made much of the new preacher. The wealth of that larger population enabled Conway to establish several charitable homes. He married there Ellen Davis Dana, and there published his first book, "Tracts For Today." He edited a paper, The Dial, to which Emerson contributed.

He went to England to the South Place Chapel, London, an ethical society, and the round peg seemed to have found its proper hole at last. Here he labored for twenty years, and became known through all Europe. His personal recollections of Alfred Tennyson, the Brownings their courtship: of Carlyle, are classics. A very interesting light is thrown on

He Travels Through Russia

Freud. He was intimate with the whole pre-Raphaelite school and gives account among others of Rossetti and his lovely wife, all friendships he formed in Madam Brown's charming home.

Burne Jones, Morris, Whistler, Swinburne, Arthur Hughs, DeMaurier (was there ever such a collection of genius in one country) are all described in Conway's vivid pen pictures. Artemus Warde was his friend, and Conway conducted the funeral services over that world's joy giver, and in his same South End Chapel, preached memorial addresses on Cobblen, Dickens, Maurice, Mazzanni, Mill, Straus, Livingstone, George Eliot, Stanley, Darwin, Longfellow, Carlyle, the beloved Emerson, Tennyson, Huxley and Abe Lincoln, whom he never admired, though he recognized his brain and personality. He accused him of precipitating the horrible war for the sake of a flag and thus murdering a million men.

Samuel Clemens (Mark Twain) and his wife visited England in 1872 and Moncure Conway and his wife knew them intimately and afterwards visited them in this country. Joseph Jefferson, John Motley, George Eliot, Mrs. Humphrey Ward (whose book, Robert Elsmere, he flays) and W. S. Gilbert, all were his friends The man was a genius, a social Voltaire; a master of thought and phrase. Where before did an exile from his own country ever achieve a friendship circle where the names now scintillate over all the world?

He visited Paris in 1867 and the story of his travels in Russia later are full of charm, of folk lore and religious mysticism. But before long we find him back in his South Place Chapel. His accounts of several woman preachers there are interesting, as is that of Annie Besant—the wondrous before-her-time—whom Mrs. Conway befriended in her bitter persecution by her parson husband for agnosticism. In 1875 Conway returned to America, and Falmouth town, grieving over the war ravages and his lost boyhood friends. He toured through the West, lecturing on Demonology, and the great Englishmen he knew. The death of his son, Dana, and of his wife in 1897, were blows,

Beautiful "Belmont"
On Falmouth Heights, Now the Home of Mr. and Mrs. Gari Melchers

A Great American Artist

and his remaining years were spent in Europe with several visits between to his brother, Peter V. D. Conway, of Fredericksburg, and friends in America. His life ended in 1907 in Paris. A great man, a brilliant and a brave one. He fought for his beliefs as bravely as ever did any warrior or explorer in unknown lands.

GARI MELCHERS

Crowning a hill, which is the triumphant result of a series of terraces rising from the town of Falmouth, opposite Fredericksburg, is Belmont, the home of Gari Melchers, an American artist, who has been more honored abroad than any of our living painters, with the exception, perhaps, of John Singer Sargent.

Born in Detroit, Gari Melchers left America when he was seventeen, to pursue his studies in Europe.

His apprentice days were spent in Dusseldorf and Paris, where his professional debut in 1889 gained for him the coveted Grand Prix — Sargent and Whistler being the only other American painters similarly honored.

Italy had to resign to Holland the prestige of lending her country to the genius of Mr. Melchers, for he intended to reside in Italy, but owing to the outbreak of the cholera there he settled at Engmond instead. His studio borrowed the interest of the sea on one side and the charm of a lazy canal on the other, and over its door were inscribed the words: "Wahr und Klar" (Truth and Clarity). Here he worked at those objective and realistic pictures of Dutch life and scenes; and free from all scholastic pretense, he painted the serene, yet colorful panorama of Holland.

Christian Brinton says of the art of Gari Melchers that it is explicit and veracious. Prim interiors are permeated with a light that envelopes all things with a note of sadness. Exterior scenes reflect the shifting of seasons or the precise hour of day. He paints air as well as light and color. Without

John Elder's Great Work

exaggeration, he manages to suggest the intervening aerial medium between the seer and the thing seen.

Mr. Melchers has no set formula.

In 1918 there was a wonderful "one man" display of his art at the Corcoran Art Gallery, and in 1919, the Loan Exhibition, held by the Copley Society at the Boston Art Club, was the second of the two important recent events in the artist's career since his returning to America. Here his work has undergone some perceptible change, gaining lightness and freshness of vision, which shows his reaction to a certain essential Americanism. Mr. Melchers attacks whatever suits his particular mood, and his art is not suggestive of a subjective temperament.

"The Sermon"—"The Communion"—"The Pilots"—"The Shipbuilders"—"The Sailor and His Sweetheart"—"The Open Door" are some of his well-known canvases. His reputation as a portrait painter rests upon a secure foundation.

His awards include medals from Berlin, Antwerp, Vienna, Paris and Munich, Ansterdam, Dresden, Pennsylvania Academy of Fine Arts, and many other medals for art exhibitions.

He is an officer of the Legion of Honor, France; officer of the Order of the "Red Eagle," Prussia; officer of the Order of "St. Michael" Bavaria; officer of the Order of the "White Falcon," Saxe-Weimar.

Mr. Melchers himself is frank and not chained by minor conventions. He has a powerful personality and a charming wife, who dispenses a pleasant hospitality, in a home that leaves nothing to be desired.

John A. Elder

Fredericksburg gave John A. Elder, the gifted painter to the world, for he saw the light of day in this town in February, 1833; and here he first felt that call to art which had its beginnings when Elder would, as a mere boy, make chalk drawings

Some of Elder's Paintings

on the sides of the buildings, and took the time, while doing errands for his father, to give rein to his imagination through some interesting sketch, which would finally drift into the possession of his friends. His father's opposition to an artistic career for his son did not long retard his progress, as so great was the urge within him that he borrowed from a fellow townsman, Mr. John Minor, the money to study abroad, and before long Dusseldorf, Germany, claimed him as a student, and there the love of line and color which he had inherited from his mother's family gained definition. Details of his life in Dusseldorf are too vague to chronicle but he returned to this country at the beginning of the Civil War, with a knowledge of his art which gained him instant recognition, and success followed in his footsteps.

Elder was a man whose sympathetic personality drew the love of his fellow-men, and his studio was the rendezvous of such men as Attorney-General R. T. Daniel, Lord Grant, Peterkin, Fred Daniel, who represented the United States as consul to Rome for fourteen years, and many others.

His experiences in war gave to him a sureness and truth in detail, which, when added to his technique, produced results which challenged the admiration of all who saw his work.

His "Battle of the Crater" and "Scout's Prize" were inspired by scenes in which he had figured. The former hangs on the walls of the Westmoreland Club, in Richmond, Va., and his canvas "After Appomattox" adorns the State Library in the same city, along with many portraits which trace their origin to him.

His "Lee" and "Jackson" are in the Corcoran Art Gallery in Washington, and there is a portrait of Mr. Corcoran himself which owes its existence to his gifted brush.

He visited Jefferson Davis at "Beauvoir" and painted him there.

Of ordinary height and rather thick set, Mr. Elder's appearance was characterized by distinction and force. His eyes were dark and very expressive; he wore a moustache and "imperial" and in all his photographs we notice the "artistic flowing tie" On the left of his forehead was a scar, the result of some encounter in Germany, and as the artist never married, one is apt to read a romance into his life. However, this is pure speculation, as there is nothing to substantiate such an assumption.

"Jack" Elder was a master of the foils, and on one occasion when a noted Frenchman engaged him in a "bout" Elder disarmed him with ease, and the Frenchman's foil was thrown against the ceiling.

The artist returned to Fredericksburg, where he lived six years prior to his death, which occurred on February 25, 1895, and in these last years he was ministered to by his nieces and nephews, who showed him much devotion.

Rev. James Power Smith

Rev. James Power Smith was not born in Fredericksburg, but he preached here for thirty years, at the Presbyterian Church, aiding the poor and sick, and always smiling. He was highly successful in his church achievements and in his years of editorship of the Central Presbyterian.

One night in his life proved him to be minted of fine metal, and that night inscribed his name forever in history. It was the fearful night when Stonewall Jackson received his death blow.

Captain Smith (now Reverend) was a theological student when war broke out, and was immediately made a military lieutenant (not a chaplain). Throughout the war he followed close to Jackson, on his staff. Religion brought them together and their friendship was deep.

When in the darkness of the trees that overhang the Chancellorsville road, "Stonewall" Jackson was mortally wounded and others about him killed by their own troops there were a few men, among them General A. P. Hill, at hand to help him. He had hardly been taken from his horse when two aides,

Lieutenant Morrison and Lieutenant Smith, arrived. With General Hill directing, they arrested the bleeding. General Hill had to hurry back to form his men for an attack. Lieutenant Morrison had just seen a field piece, not 200 yards away, pointing down the Plank Road. There was no litter, and General Jackson offered to walk to the rear. Leaning on Major Leigh and Lieutenant Morrison, he began struggling toward his lines. They had just placed Jackson on a litter that had been sent up, when the Federal cannon began to rake the road with canister. Every figure, horse or gun toward the Confederate lines disappeared. They tried to take him back, but a litter-bearer was struck down and the Great Leader was dropped and bruised.

In a moment, on the dark road swept by awful fire, there were but three men, and, as the subject of this sketch, Lieutenant Smith, was one of them, it is apropos to quote what Prof. R. S. Dabney says in his Life of Jackson:

"The bearers and all the attendants, excepting Major Leigh and the general's two aides, had left and fled into the woods. While the sufferer lay in the road with his feet turned toward the enemy, exposed to the fire of the guns, his attendants displayed a heroic fidelity which deserved to go down in history with the immortal name of Jackson. Disdaining to leave their chief, they lay down beside him, leaning above him and trying as far as possible to protect him with their bodies. On one side was Major Leigh, on the other Lieutenant Smith. Again and again was the earth torn by volleys of canister, and minnie balls hissed over them, the iron striking flashes from the stones about him."

Finally when the firing ceased, General Jackson was removed from the battlefield to a hospital, and then to Mr. Chandler's house at Guinea Station, where he died, May 10, 1863.

Lieutenant Smith became The Reverend when war ceased, and married Miss Agnes Lucy Lacy, a daughter of Major J. Horace Lacy.

Major J. Horace Lacy

He was well known in Fredericksburg. For thirty years he was pastor here; for fifty years Secretary of the Presbyterian Synod, and for years editor of the Central Presbyterian. Many know his works. All men know the deep, immovable courage it took that night to lie as a barrier, to take whatever death might be hurled down the shell-swept road toward "Stonewall" Jackson.

He still lives, in 1921, in Richmond. His voice is low, his smile soft, and his religion his life. He is the last survivng member of "Stonewall" Jackson's staff.

Major J. Horace Lacy

There are many living now who remember him. The strong, stolid figure, the fine old face traced with the lineage of gentility, the cane that pounded down the sidewalks as he went where he willed. There are some left who knew the power and poetry and kindliness of the man.

Major Lacy was a graduate of Washington and Lee and an attorney at law, though he seldom practiced. He was married in 1848 at Chatham, when he was twenty-four years of age, to Miss Betty Churchill Jones, and later became the owner of "Chatham" and of the "Lacy House," about each of which clings grim traditions of war; both the Wilderness place and Chatham became known in those two battles as "The Lacy House."

Washington Irving was his guest while spending some time in Virginia; General Robert E. Lee was his guest, and many other widely known men.

His service in war was well done. He was made a lieutenant at the beginning and promoted to major on the field of battle at Seven Pines. He served under General Joseph E. Johnston until the latter surrendered, some time after Appomattox.

When the war was ended he went North to do a brave thing. He spoke through Pennsylvania and Maryland, plead-

Winning a Hostile Audience

ing for funds to bury and put grave stones over the Confederate dead. He had experiences there. But his splendid oratory and the courage of his presence usually kept order.

He spoke once at Baltimore, and among his audience was an Irish Federal regiment, clad half in uniform, half in civilians, as forgotten ex-privates usually are. Major Lacy was told that most of the audience was hostile and threatening.

He walked on the platform and spoke a few words about the unknown men he came to get funds to decently bury, of the women away where the starlight was twinkling over cabin and home, of those who waited, listening for a step; of those who were never again to see the men they loved.

Shuffling feet and laughter dulled the simple pathos of his words. Then turning half away from his audience he recited a poem called "The Irish Immigrant's Lament":

> "I am sitting on the stile, Mary,
> Where we sat, side by side,
> On that bright May morning long ago,
> When first you were my bride."

He began it thus, and into his voice, filled with the sorrows of the "Mary's" who wept down in his Southland, he put the full strength of his expression. The hostile audience was silent as he finished.

> And often in the far-off world,
> I'll sit and close my eyes,
> And my heart will travel back again
> To where my Mary lies.
> And I'll think I see the little stile
> Where we sat, side by side,
> Mid the young corn on that bright May morn
> When you were first my bride."

The Irishmen who had fought against the cause which Lacy loved were quiet now, and when he said, "Wouldn't you want a bit of a stone for 'Mary' to remember you," they yelled and rushed to grasp his hand. From his "hostile" audience he collected $14,000.00 that night. In the whole tour he gathered a great sum for Confederate cemeteries.

During his later years, with his wife, who represented the ladies of another era, as he did its men, he lived on Washington Avenue, in Fredericksburg. To few did he ever show the deeper side of his character, but those who knew him until he died in 1906, knew how much kindly manliness dwelt therein.

Major General Daniel Ruggles

Although Major General Daniel Ruggles was born in Massachusetts, he married Miss Richardetta Mason Hooe, a great granddaughter of George Mason, and the greater part of his life was spent in Fredericksburg, of which he became a citizen and in which he died.

During his life in Fredericksburg he concerned himself with the business of the town, and was known to almost all of its residents.

He was graduated into the army from West Point in 1883 and lead a small band into the west and explored the Fox river the same year.

When the Seminole Indian war broke out Lieutenant Ruggles with fifty men penetrated the everglades and was commended for his services. In the Mexican war he stopped the Mexican advance at Palo Alto and was promoted to Captain on the field.

Captain Ruggles and his men reached Chapaultepec, drove into the city, made a determined stand and were the first of the advancing American Army to raise the American flag over the fort. He was breveted Major by President Polk "for gallant and meritorious conduct at Chereubusco" and a little later was made Lieutenant Colonel "for gallant and conspicuous bravery at Chapaultepec." In 1861 he joined the Confederate Army.

Placed in command of the most important of the Southern departments at Fredericksburg, the "gateway to the

Old "Chatham"
One of the Most Characteristic of All Virginia Colonial Mansions

The Real "First Battle"

South," he organized and equipped a small army. When the Confederacy found that they had no gun caps, necessary on the old "muzzle loaders," and no copper from which to make caps, General Ruggles invented a cap made from raw hide and dried in the sun (specimens are in the National Museum), which were used by the whole Southern Army during the first three months of the war.

General Ruggles planted artillery and, using these caps with match heads to explode them, drove off the Union gunboats and a lading force at Aquia Creek May 31, 1861, nine days before "Big Bethel", and weeks after Virginia seceded. He thus fought and won the first battle of the Civil war.

His career during the war won him wide recognition. His movements won the battle of Shiloh through finding a weak point in the enemy's line. He was made Major General March 25, 1865, and surrendered at Augusta, Ga., after Appomattox. Although he fought in five Indian wars, the Mexican war and the Civil war, from the start to finish, and was recognized as a man who would lead his men anywhere, he never received a wound of any kind in his life.

Many people in Fredericksburg remember him now, with his fine face, his erect figure and his long gray whiskers. In his latter days some people laughed at him, not understanding that there was genius in the man, because of his first experience with "rainmaking." He invented the method which is used now by the United States Government, under his patent. He earned the name of "raincrow" which sometimes reached his ears. He patented the first propeller which was ever used on a steam boat (model in the National Museum). He also invented the first principles of the telephone. He invented in 1858 a system whereby an electric bell on a ship would ring on the approach of the ship to any rock or point on the shore equipped with the same apparatus. This was tested by the navy and proclaimed impractical, but it contained the principles of wireless telegraphy. It is used by the American navy today.

Roger Clark—Major Braxton

JOHN ROGER CLARK, EXPLORER

Though a monument has just been erected in another city which claims him as a citizen, there is excellent evidence of the fact that John Roger Clarke, reclaimer of the great Northwest, and also his brother, William Clarke, who with Merriweather Lewis, explored the Mississippi, were born in Spotsylvania County and lived near Fredericksburg. According to Quinn's History of Fredericksburg, Maury's History of Virginia and letters from descendents, the two famous Clarke brothers were sons of Jonathan Clarke, who lived at Newmarket, Spotsylvania County, where John Roger Clarke was born. Jonathan Clarke was clerk of the County Court of Spotsylvania and afterwards moved to Fredericksburg, where it may be probable, the younger son was born. Later they moved to Albemarle County, near Charlottesville, where the two sons grew to manhood.

The history of the two Clarkes' is so well known, even by school children, that it is needless to go into it here, the purpose of this reference being to establish their connection with the town.

MAJOR ELLIOTT MUSE BRAXTON

Major Elliott Muse Braxton is widely known, as he was once Congressman from this district. He was born in the County of Middlesex, October 2, 1823, was a grandson of Carter Braxton, one of Virginia's signers of the Declaration of Independence. His father was also Carter Braxton, a successful lawyer in Richmond.

In 1851 he was elected to the Senate of Virginia. So ably and efficiently did Major Braxton represent his constituents that he won another election without any opposition.

In 1854 he married Anna Marie Marshall, a granddaughter of the great expounder of the Constitution, Chief Justice Marshall. In 1859 he adopted Fredericksburg as his home, where he was when "war's dread alarm," came. He organized a company of infantry, of which he was unanimously elected captain, from which position he was soon promoted to that of major, and assigned to the staff of General John R. Cooke. On the conclusion of hostilities he again engaged in the practice of law, forming a co-partnership with the late C. Wistar Wallace, Esq. In 1870 he was nominated at Alexandria by the Democrats for Congress, the City of Fredericksburg being then a constituent of the Eighth District.

He continued to practice his profession of law until failing health admonished him to lay its burdens down.

On October 2, 1891, he died in his home at Fredericksburg, and Virginia mourned a son who was always true, loyal and faithful. Elliott Muse Braxton was a Virginia gentleman and in saying that a good deal is comprehended. Courteous in manner, considerate in tone and temper, clean in character, loyal to State and to Church, cherishing with ardor as the years went by, the obligations and the responsibilities of old Virginia, he fell asleep.

Dr. Francis P. Wellford

"But a certain Samaritan as he journeyed came where he was and when he saw him, he had compassion on him — and went to him and bound up his wounds". In this way we are told the tender story of the Good Samaritan.

In 1877 Dr. Francis Preston Wellford, of Fredericksburg, was living in Jacksonville, Florida, when a scourge of yellow fever invaded Fernandina. Almost all of its physicians were victims of the disease, or worn out with work. Dr. Wellford volunteered for service, which was almost certain death, fell a victim, and died, on the same day and in the next cot to his fellow-townsman, Dr. Herndon.

> "For whether on the scaffold high,
> Or in the battle's van,
> The noblest death that man can die;
> Is when he dies for man."

Doctor James C. Herndon

Over his grave in the cemetery at Fredericksburg, there is an imposing monument, with this simple inscription:

"Francis Preston Wellford,
Born in Fredericksburg, Virginia,
September 12, 1839."

On the beautiful memorial window in St. Peter's Church, Fernandina, Florida, erected by Dr. J. H. Upham, of Boston, who felt that their memory should not be neglected, one reads:

"Francis Preston Wellford, M. D.
Born in Fredericksburg, Virginia,
Sept. 12, 1839,

James Carmicheal Herndon, M. D.
Born in Fredericksburg, Virginia,
Sept. 22, 1821,
Died in the faithful discharge of their duties at
Fernandina, Florida,
Oct. 18, 1877."

Dr. James C. Herndon

When surgeons were needed for the Confederate Army, the Dr. Herndon above mentioned left his practice and went, although exempted by law. He served through four years of war, and when peace was declared, made his home in Florida.

He was state physician there, when Fernandina was stricken by the dread yellow fever, and the population was almost helpless.

Deeming it his duty, Herndon voluntarily went into the city of the dying. He had worked but a few days when he was stricken, and death followed.

He died as bravely as a man may die, and few have died for so good a cause. He sleeps in the silent cemetery in Fredericksburg, his home.

Hon. A. Wellington Wallace

Among the men whose writings have added to Fredericksburg's fame is Hon. A. Wellington Wallace, at one time Judge of the Corporation Court of Fredericksburg and, later chosen President of the Virginia Bar Association. Judge Wallace never sought political office and his abilities therefore never were fully publicly known in that line, but some of his literary compositions have been widely read and favorably criticised. The most important of his work, perhaps, is his epitome on the intents, purposes and meaning of the constitution. Though brief it clearly and sharply defines and analyses the important document under which we are governed, and gives to the reader an intelligent conception of what its framers aimed at and hoped to do, such as could not be gained in pages of lengthier reading.

Hon. A. P. Rowe
(1817-1900)

One of the best known and most beloved characters of the after-the-war period was Absalom P. Rowe, affectionately known as "Marse Ab." He served as Quartermaster, Confederate States Army, throughout the Civil War, and after its close, played a leading part in restoring order and system out of the terrible desolation with which this section was inflicted. He was prominent in all matters pertaining to the civic and State governments and was a powerful influence in all the stirring events of that period.

"Marse Ab" represented the district comprising Fredericksburg and Spotsylvania county in the State Legislature for the session 1879-1880, and served as Mayor of Fredericksburg continuously from 1888 to 1900, with the exception of one term, and had just been re-elected for another term at the time of his death.

Fredericksburg was then under its old charter and the police court was presided over by the Mayor. "Marse Ab's"

A Famous "Tramp Comedian"

court was known far and wide, and his characteristic method of dealing out justice was the cause of fear to offenders and a source of amusement to large numbers of onlookers who always attended the sessions of court. "Marse Ab's" decisions were quickly reached and swiftly delivered, and the penalties inflicted were tempered with the wisdom and discretion of his long experience and his rare qualities as a judge of human nature.

Mayor Rowe was the father of Captain M. B. Rowe, who now owns and occupies historic Marye's Heights (see illustration facing page 52), ex-Mayor J. P. Rowe, Messrs. A. P. Rowe and Alvin T. Rowe, all prominent business men of the city today.

Nat C. Wills

Not only has Fredericksburg contributed men who took high rank in the political, economic and scientific up-building of the country, but it has furnished at least one of those who ranked highest as an amuser of the Nation. This was Nat Wills, nationally known to the American theater going public as the foremost exemplifier of the tramp. Wills' real name was Matthew McGrath Wills. When still a young man he went from Fredericksburg and made his home in Washington. There he humbly began a stage career as a tramp comedian that ended, when he was at the pinnacle of success, with his sudden death in New York some eight years ago.

Merely to have been a successful "Tramp Comedian" does not imply fame. But Wills was more than merely a tramp comedian. He was creator of a new art on the American stage and those who now caricature the lowly denizen of the cross ties, are followers of the lead he took. In mannerism, type and action they copy Wills' conception of what a true tramp should be, but none yet has succeeded in portraying the character with the humor that Wills put into his work.

Technically speaking Wills was a low comedian, but his wit and humor and art are not suggested by that term. Dressed

JOHN PAUL JONES HOME
Above: A Grocery Since 1760. Below, Stevens House

The Gallant Herndon's Death

in clothes that were themselves a burlesque of the world's kindness, he represented with dramatic humor a character that went through life unconscious of his rags, careless of the present and unafraid of the future, but with a kindness of heart and a philosophy that is true only to those who have viewed life from close to its rougher aspects. After he had achieved success his plays were especially written for him and he had a large part in their making. His lines were witty and clever and as curtain encores he sang parodies he had written on whatever were the popular songs of the day, and these were brilliant satires on the original themes.

Wills never forgot the city of his nativity. Whenever close enough to be appreciated, he always told a joke that permitted him to bring in his connection with the town. His sudden death was a shock to theater goers, and no one has since supplanted in their affections the particular character he essayed. Though dead he remains master of the art he created.

Commander Wm. Lewis Herndon

It is not so much because of his life as of his death, that every Fredericksburger cherishes the memory of Commander William Lewis Herndon. He was born here in 1813, and fifteen years afterwards was made a midshipman and in 1855 reached the rank of Admiral. Commander Herndon made the first exploration of the Amazon, amidst great dangers, and his book on this subject became a standard.

With 478 souls aboard, Commander Herndon started from New York for South America in 1857 on the big passenger ship "Central America." She sailed proudly out, the flying fish fleeing her prow down the Gulf Stream through sunny days, until suddenly in the Gulf of Mexico the ship shattered against a rock.

Standing with his sword in his hand, Commander Herndon saw the boats lowered one by one until each woman and child was safely on the sea in life boats. Ordering his men to continue disembarking passengers he went below to put on his dress uniform, and coming back directed the making of rafts. Hundreds of men jumped and nearly 150 were lost. Commander Herndon stood last on the ship upon the Bridge that is a Captain's castle, the gold of his uniform losing its glow as the sun fell behind the far off shore lines. Still hovering near, the sailors in a half dozen boats in which were women and children, cried out to him to come over. He bent his head a moment in prayer then doffed his cocked hat, and smiling, went down as his ship plunged bow forward into the Gulf waters. There is no tradition of our Navy more glowing than this one, which Commander Herndon, of Fredericksburg, added to its legends.

Captain Rudd, U. S. Navy

Captain John Rudd was a resident of our City after his retirement from the U. S. Navy. He was too old to serve in the Confederacy and lived in a house next to the old Citizens Hall, near where the Catholic Church now stands.

He sailed many years in the old Navy, and had many tales to tell to the young people of his neighborhood concerning his adventures.

Commodore Theo. R. Rootes

Commodore Theo. R. Rootes resigned from the U. S. Navy in 1861, and was immediately named as commander in the Confederate Navy. He was stationed in Richmond in the early part of the war and in 1864 was given the command of the ironclad "Fredericksburg" of the James river fleet. He took part in the expedition against the U. S. fleet on the James river and was a member of the Naval Brigade which after the evacuation of Richmond was surrounded at Sailors Creek, April 6, 1865. He lived in the old Scott house, now owned by Charles Cole, Esq., on the corner of Prince Edward and Amelia Streets.

Two Great Naval Officers

Rear Admiral Griffin

Of the men whom Fredericksburg has sent forth in its more modern era, Rear Admiral Robert S. Griffin, who was born in 1857, entered as a cadet engineer at Annapolis and was graduated in 1878, is among the most notable. Admiral Griffin has spent no fewer than fourteen years of a busy career on sea duty, and has been for a decade a recognized authority on naval engineering. In his position as Chief of the Bureau of Naval Engineering he is responsible for the innovations and improvements in our capital ships, the electric drive for cruisers, the turbine reduction gear for destroyers.

The high state of efficiency in the Engineering Department is due to Admiral Griffin's constant efforts and his tact in overcoming Naval and Congressional opposition is a personal accomplishment.

Admiral Griffin resigned from the Bureau on September 21, 1921, and was retired September 27, 1921.

He lives in Washington, but is a valued visitor to his former City from time to time. Admiral Griffin's record is almost unexcelled. He rose by hard work and brains and has for years been a source of pride to Fredericksburg. He is one of the few men still living whom we may class as "great."

Captain Barney, U. S. Navy

Captain Joseph N. Barney was born in Baltimore in 1818. He graduated from Annapolis first in his class in 1834 and spent many years at sea until 1861, when he resigned to offer his services to the Confederacy.

He commanded the "Jamestown" at the Battle of Hampton Roads, March 8th and 9th, 1862, and, on April 11th, was sent in to capture vessels under the guns of the Monitor, hoping to provoke the latter to come out and fight.

He commanded a battery at the fight at Drury's Bluff, and later in the war took part in the operations at the Sabine pass and was sent to command the C. S. Cruiser Florida, but was prevented by ill health. He was purchasing agent for the Confederacy at the cessation of the hostilities, and after the war made one voyage in the command of a commercial steamer. Captain Barney made his home in Fredericksburg from 1874 to 1899, when his death occurred. His career was a distinguished one and he had in his later years, spent here, a host of friends in Fredericksburg.

CAPTAIN LYNCH, U. S. NAVY

Captain M. F. Lynch was born near Fredericksburg, in 1801 was appointed a midshipman in the U. S. Navy in 1819, promoted to Lieutenant in 1828, and shortly afterwards made an important scientific investigation of the topography of the Dead Sea Valley in Palestine. He made the first correct maps and soundings of the Jordan and the Dead Sea, and his report was published by the United States Government and much valued by the scientific world. He was made a Captain in 1856 and held this rank when he resigned to enter the Confederate Navy. His work with the Virginia Navy in the defenses of Aquia Creek and the Potomac was complimented by his opponents, and later he took part in the defense of the coast of North Carolina, winning much credit by his zealous action at the battles of Hatteras Inlet and Roanoke Island.

In 1864 Captain Lynch was transferred to duty on the Mississippi River, where he aided in the preparation of the famous ram, the Arkansas, for her brilliant career. He died in Baltimore, October 17, 1865.

COMMANDER GEORGE MINOR, C. S. N.

Commander George Minor resigned from the United States Navy in April, 1861, and was immediately put in command of the newly created Bureau of Ordinance and Hydrography at Richmond. This Bureau was of invaluable service to the young Confederacy, sending out 220 guns in the first year. Commander Minor was instrumental in establishing the arsenals at Atlanta and New Orleans and other points. He spent his last years in our City, well remembered by many of the present generation. He died in 1878. While residing in Fredericksburg he lived in what was the late College Building.

Commander Robert D. Thorburn

Commander Robert D. Thorburn was a member of the old Naval Service, coming to Virginia in 1861, and being at once named to take part in the defenses of the Potomac under Captain Lynch. He later was detailed to duty on the Gulf Coast, and after the war came to Fredericksburg where he died in 1883. He resided in the house on lower Princess Anne Street, now occupied by W. D. Scott, Esq.

Major Edward Ruggles

Major Edward Ruggles was graduated from Annapolis in 1859, came South in 1861 and offered his services to the State of Virginia, before that State joined the Confederacy. He was later transferred to the Confederate Army, and served on the staff of General Daniel S. Ruggles in the engagements at Aquia Creek, being present at the first engagement of the Civil War, June 1, 1861. Later he served with the Army of Tennessee and after the war lived in King George and Fredericksburg, where he died in 1919, at his residence on lower Main Street.

Colonel Richard L. Maury

Colonel Richard L. Maury, a son of Commodore Matthew Fontaine Maury, was born in Fredericksburg in 1840. Upon the outbreak of the War between the States he at once offered his services to his native State, and his Naval Career, though short, is notable. Detached from Company F, Richmond, 1st Va. Regiment, by order of the Secretary of the Navy, he took part in the capture of the St. Nicholas and other vessels on the Potomac and Chesapeake. He was afterwards returned to the Army and served with the 24th Va. Infantry until Appomattox. After the War he resided in Lexington and Richmond, in which latter city he died a few years ago.

COMMODORE DORNIN

Commodore Thomas Dornin, U. S. N., like many other officers of the old Navy, often left his family in Fredericksburg while absent on the long tours of sea duty, sometimes two and even three years in length. Thus, while a native of Ireland, where he was born in 1801, Commodore Dornin called our town "home" for many years.

Entering the U. S. Navy in 1818, after many voyages to all parts of the world he was with Admiral Perry when the latter forced his way into the Japanese harbors. When the war between the States was imminent, he retained his place in the old Navy, with the promise that he would not be ordered to action against his adopted State.

He served on the Light House Board at Baltimore for the duration of the war, and upon his retirement in 1870 lived in Fredericksburg, for a time. He died in Savannah, Ga., in 1873.

He resided, when in Fredericksburg, in the house now owned by Dr. C. Mason Smith on Prince Edward Street.

WILLIAM HENRY BECK

Surgeon William Henry Beck, U. S. Navy, came to Virginia from England as a lad of twelve in 1800. Some years later he entered the Navy as an Assistant Surgeon, and made several voyages in the old sailing ships to various ports of the world.

He married Miss England, of Stafford, and made his home in Fredericksburg.

He lived in what was then a northwestern suburb, near the present basin, and this section was known as "Becksville." He was at one time a police officer in our town, and as the result of an injury in arresting a prisoner, lost an arm.

He died in the fifties, and was buried in St. George's Churchyard. A son bought and lived for years on what is known by our old citizens as "Beck's Island," now owned and occupied by Mr. J. A. Emery.

JOHN RANDOLPH BRYAN

Lieutenant John Randolph Bryan, U. S. Navy, born in 1806, in Georgia, was educated in Virginia, and married at Chatham in 1830, Elizabeth Coalter, daughter of Judge John Coalter, of the Virginia Supreme Court. Leaving Yale in 1823, Lieutenant Bryan was appointed to the Navy, became midshipman in 1824, and was ordered to the Peacock.

He resigned in 1831 and took charge of his estate at Wilmington Island, and later an estate in Gloucester County, Virginia.

In 1862, he offered his services to the Confederate Navy, but was judged too old. He was the ward of John Randolph, who made a deep impression upon his mentality.

Lieutenant Bryan was noted for his courtesy and charm of manner. He spent his latter years in the house of his daughter in Fredericksburg, Mrs. Spotswood W. Carmichael. He died at the University of Virginia, while on a visit, on September 13, 1887.

The name of Mrs. Spotswood W. Carmichael will recall to many Dr. Carmichael, that splendid physician and gentleman of "the old school" who ministered to the sick of a previous generation and had a host of loyal friends.

Captain Reuben Thom, C. S N.

CAPTAIN THOM, U. S. M. C.

Captain Reuben Thom, of the Confederate Marine Corps, was the son of "Postmaster Thom" and was born in Fredericksburg. He entered the war at Norfolk in 1861, and in 1862 was in command of the Marines on the famous Merrimac in the battle of Hampton Roads. Captain Thom took part in the engagement at Drury's Bluff. After the war Captain Thom moved to Baltimore where he died.

BETTY WASHINGTON'S HOME
*"Kenmore" Where George Washington's Sister Lived After Her Marriage.
Her Mother's Home is Close By*

Unforgotten Women

Some of Many Who Left a Record of Brilliancy, Service or Sacrifice.

The stars that shine in the galaxy of the heavens do not all glow with the same lustre. One is gifted with a steady and dependable splendor, another scintillates and fades to shine afresh. So, it is, that the women of Fredericksburg have in their individual ways added to the glories of the town and well sustained its deserved reputation, as being the home of capable, brilliant, and beautiful women. A distinguished French officer once said, after meeting one of the women of Fredericksburg, "If such are the matrons of America, well may she boast of illustrious sons." This was at the great Peace Ball, given in the town in 1783, to which, of course, the mother of Washington was especially invited. The simple manner and appearance of the great woman, surprised the gallant officers present, and provoked from one of them the remark.

Clad in a plain but becoming garb, that characterized Virginia women of her type, she received the many attentions paid to the Mother of the idolized Commander-in-Chief with the most unaffected dignity and courtesy. Being accustomed to the pomp and splendor which is attached to Old World royalty, it was a revelation to them to behold such a woman. How could she live in the blaze of glory which irradiated her illustrious offspring, and still preserve her simple dignity of manner, so barren of self pride and hauteur!

But this daughter of Colonel Joseph Ball, of Lancaster County, this "Rose of Epping Forest" which budded into existence on March 6, 1708, this unassuming woman, who on the anniversary of her natal day in 1730, gave her heart and hand to the master of Wakefield, this thrifty and systematic young housewife and widowed mother at Pine Grove, in Stafford County, this matron of Fredericksburg, possessed qualities

The "Rose of Epping Forest"

individual to her who became the author of the being of the greatest and best loved character figuring on the pages of American history. Her last home selected for her by General Washington, stands today, on the corner of Charles and Lewis Streets, the same home with the characteristic simplicity of years ago. The Association for the Preservation of Virginia Antiquities, to which Society it now belongs, has restored in part the interior with its wainscoting and paneling and its period furniture. The interesting old brick floored kitchen, with its hugh fireplace, and its crane, iron pots, skillets and equipment of former days, all seem today in perfect accord with her reception of her cherished offspring in 1783. After an enforced cessation of visits to his aging mother for a long period of seven years, she at length was told by an orderly that "His Excellency" had arrived, and was at her very door. Turning quietly to her faithful, ebony maid, she said with her habitual self control, "Patsy, George has come, I shall need a white apron." But beneath this calm exterior, her embrace of her first born son was overflowing with fervent mother-love, and hidden away in the deep recesses of her heart was the swelling pride in his glory. Senator Daniel truthfully said, "The principles which he applied to a nation were those simple and elementary truths which she first imprinted upon his mind in the discipline of home."

The splendid granite monument, erected to her, with its simple inscription, "Mary, the Mother of Washington," and on the reverse side: "Erected by her Countrywomen," rises from a massive foundation to a distance of 59 feet. Her ashes lie beneath, in a spot of her own selection, (which in her lifetime was a part of the Kenmore estate) and her favorite resting place. Nearby are the two rocks upon which she used to sit and read her Bible. These are known as Meditation Rocks."

The name of Susan Metcalf Savage will always be held in the highest veneration by those of Fredericksburg who realize and appreciate the many sacrifices, heart-aches, self-

Susan Savage and Anne Maury

denials and home-longings experienced by those who give their lives in heathen lands. Brought up in an atmosphere of love and unselfishness, and herself devoted to every call of duty, it was no surprise to her many friends to learn that soon after her marriage to Reverend Dr. Savage in 1838 she would sail with him for tropical Africa, one of the first woman missionaries from our land. Though her life in this then unusual field of usefulness was less than two short years, her labors were not in vain, and her works and her example will live for years to come.

Ann Herndon, who became the wife of the great scientist, Matthew Fontaine Maury, was born in the house on the corner of Princess Anne and George Streets, erected by her father, Dabney M. Herndon. Her loveliness of face and character was equalled by her charming manner, and attractive personality, and whether in Fredericksburg, or Lexington, Va., whether in Washington or London, her home was the spot where the savant, the scientist, the literati and men and women representing every phase of culture and social distinction, were wont to assemble. The beautiful jewels presented to her by the crowned heads of Europe, (her illustrious husband, being an officer in the United States Navy, was restricted from accepting gifts, else his admirers would have showered them upon him), were deservedly famous. After the death of Commodore Maury a plan was conceived by a member of one of the royal courts of Europe, and initiatory steps had already been taken, to raise a munificent sum of mony with which to honor the widow of the man to whom all educated nations were to pay homage. But when their project reached her ear, she refused to accept it, though recognizing and appreciating fully the compliment to her devoted husband.

One of the captivating belles of the town was Ellen Lewis Herndon, daughter of the Naval Commander, Captain William Lewis Herndon, who in 1857 met his death in the Gulf

President Arthur's Wife

Stream. Being possessed of a rich contralto voice, Miss Herndon made frequent visits to the National Capitol, and delighted the congregations at old St. John's Church with her sweet, rich tones. It was here that the young attorney, Chester A. Arthur, afterwards President, became infatuated with the pretty young singer. Those old days were the parents of these days, and many were the whispers of conjecture and surmise as to the outcome of those frequent visits of the handsome Mr. Arthur to the home of Ellen Herndon, (that still strikingly pretty residence on Main and Charlotte Streets), and shortly before the War between the States, a pretty wedding was solemnized in New York City, and Ellen Herndon became the bride of Chester A. Arthur.

In the heart-rending times of 1861-'65, the women of Fredericksburg with untiring energy and courage, in the midst of the agony of war, assumed the laborious task of ministering alike to soldiers in blue and gray, and many burdens of sorrow were in some way lightened and many a physical pain lessened or a soul cheered. Perhaps the women of Fredericksburg were inspired to great deeds by the example of that splendid specimen of womanhood, Clara Barton, who for sometime was stationed near Chatham, carrying on her splendid ministration to the sick and suffering Federal soldiers.

OF WOMAN'S WORK

It was on May 10, 1866, that the women of Fredericksburg, urged by Mrs. Frances Seymour White, (widow of an officer in the U. S. Army, who died as the war began), assembled in the lecture room of St. George's Church to form an association to care for the memory of the noble Southern heroes, whose graves were then scattered over battlefield and farm. This was the first step towards the formation of the Ladies Memorial Association the work of which organization, begun so earnestly and lovingly, has so successfully been fulfilled. Mrs. John H. Wallace, was elected President and Mrs. Frances Seymour White, Vice-President. On Mrs. Wallace's death, Mrs. White was chosen President, and continued until 1882, when she was succeeded by her daughter, Mrs. Francis B. Goolrick, who continued to act as President for eleven years. Mrs. Maria K. Daniel followed next for seventeen years, and Mrs. Frances B. Goolrick, who was elected in 1912 is still President.

With the financial assistance of about all the Southern States and a good deal from the North the bodies of the Confederate soldiers have been re-interred in the Confederate cemetery, and each is marked with a solid granite headstone. Later with some financial assistance the splendid monument "To the Confederate Dead," was erected in the center of the cemetery. The base is of gray granite, quarried in Spotsylvania County, and the life-like statue of the Confederate soldier on dress parade, which surmounts the apex, is of bronze.

The beautiful custom of Memorial Day sprang from Mrs. Frances Seymour White's idea and spread from this city all over the nation. The name of "The Ladies Memorial Assoiation" was adopted and in the Spring season each year, this impressive service is continued. Following those true hearted women who conceived the task of rescuing from oblivion the memory of those brave and fallen heroes, the United Daughters of the Confederacy, and the women of Fredericksburg branch of the American Red Cross, have each in their respective spheres, earnestly and lovingly performed their tasks.

The recent passing from our midst of the material presence of a worthy representative of the women of Fredericksburg, inspired the glowing tribute to the women of Virginia, appearing as an editorial in a local paper. The writer says in part, "We shall ever cherish the recollection that old Virginia had a womanhood of whom the people of the nation must be proud. Lest we be misunderstood we would have it known that we boast today of our womanhood and are hon-

Mary Washington Hospital

ored by those now among us; yet no one can successfully deny that the type of women of the Old Dominion of the bygone years was of an exceptional character. They were the result of the very environment in which they were born and reared. For purity of purpose, for modesty of demeanor and conversation, for unselfish devotion to home where there was real happiness, for gentleness, for refinement, for self abnegation, for love of God and the Church, for unostentatious charity, and for high motherhood, she has never had superiors. For all the essential attributes and elements which go to form a splendid woman without guile and without reproach, we hazard nothing in declaring that Virginia —in the World's Hall of Fame—gives to her womanhood of olden days her laurel of immortal glory."

Another work which will always be a tribute to woman's indefatigable and preserving efforts, is the Mary Washington Hospital, beautifully situated on the river's bank immediately facing the lawns and Terraces of Chatham, and when the trees are bare in winter, affording a view of the imposing mansion. Here, since 1897, thousands of sick have been cared for and nursed back to health and strength with more scientific care and almost as much loving attention as they could receive in their own homes. In 1897 the corner-stone was laid and from that time the Hospital has steadily grown and progressed, gaining in strength and usefulness, and now is recognized as essential to the city and surrounding counties. The idea of establishing the Hospital was originated by two or three ladies and the work put actively in motion by Mrs. W. Seymour White and Mrs. M. F. Tankard, who constituted themselves a committee to form an auxiliary society, which supported by Mr. W. Seymour White, who was at that time Mayor of the City, obtained a sufficient sum to purchase a lot and build a small house of a few rooms. A Hospital Association was formed, and the women did almost phenomenal work in struggling through many discouragements, never losing faith, but pressing forward and overcoming every

Mary Washington Monument

obstacle until their efforts were crowned with success and the Hospital established on a firm foundation. Now the few rooms have grown into a commodious building accommodating thirty or forty patients, a Nurses Home and corps of young women in training. Mrs. W. Seymour White beame the first president — elected because of her interest in establishing it, and in recognition of the strong support given it by her husband as Mayor, who in that capacity was able to weild an influence that helped materially towards its success.

The Mary Washington Monument has a history too long to be embraced in this volume and only a brief sketch of it will be appropriate. "The Building of a Monument" was written by Miss Susan Riviere Hetzel, and published in 1903. She was at the time Secretary of the National Mary Washington Memorial Association, following her mother Mrs. Margaret Hetzel, its first Secretary.

The idea of erecting a new monument to Mary Washington seemed to spring up simultaneously in Fredericksburg and in Boston, and spread like wild-fire over the country. Miss Hetzel claims priority for her mother, while the actual first published movement took place in Fredericksburg. Two letters were written and published on the same date in the Washington Post. Both letters were written in the spring just at the time of the Johnstown flood, and held in the newspaper office, probably overlooked, until October. On October 13th the movement crystalized into a large meeting in Fredericksburg. The writers of the two letters became acquainted through a mutual interest. Mrs. Goolrick's letter proposed a National Organization with a President and one Vice-President for each State. Mrs. Hetzel's letter suggested that "every woman as far as able give one dollar to the proposed monument with the Washington Post as Treasurer for the fund, and to acknowledge daily the donations received." On the appearance of the letters in the Washington Post Mrs. Hetzel wrote to Mrs. Goolrick, congratulating her on the plan she

Dedication of Monument

proposed, stating that such a plan was then practically in operation, and had been worked up during the summer, Mrs. Waite, wife of Chief Justice Waite, was made president, but they wished no publication or mention made of it until they obtained their Charter. On November 8th, 1889, the Fredericksburg Association received its Charter. The National Association was chartered February 22nd, 1890. On the 10th of May, 1894, the Mary Washington Monument was dedicated, with great form and ceremony and with the largest crowd ever gathered in Fredericksburg. Visitors flocked from all over the country. The streets were in gala attire. American, and Virginia State flags fluttered everywhere with the buff, blue and gold insignia of the Ball family, which floated before the homes of Mary Ball's decendants. A special train from Washington arrived at ten o'clock bringing the President of the United States, Grover Cleveland, the Chief Justice, members of the Cabinet and other invited guests with the ladies of the National Mary Washington Memorial Association, the Daughters of the American Revolution, and the Marine Band. Military Companies from Richmond, Alexandria and other cities were present, and with the various orders of the city made an imposing spectacle. The Grand Lodge of Masons from this and other places closed the procession, with the Grand Master of the Grand Lodge of Virginia, and the Grand Secretary of the Grand Lodge of the District of Columbia following in its wake. On the immense rostrum near the Monument were seated all the officials, and Societies, with seats reserved for the descendants of Mary Ball who were specially invited by the National Association. They had been summoned from the East and from the West, one invitation going to Japan to Paymaster Mason Ball, U. S. N.

The ceremonies opened with a prayer by Rev. James Power Smith. Mayor Rowe next welcomed on the part of the city the President, Governor and other distinguished guests. He gave a brief account of the first monument and laying of the corner stone by President Andrew Jackson, with an eloquent tribute to the Mary Washington Association and "the

MARY WASHINGTON MONUMENT
Standing at the Spot that She Selected for Her Grave. The Only Monument Built By Women to a Woman

noble women in various sections, some of whom grace this occasion by their presence today." The President of the United States was welcomed by Governor Charles T. O'Ferrall on behalf of the Commonwealth of Virginia. An impressive address was then delivered by the President. The Monument was then dedicated by the Grand Master of Masons of Virginia — Mann Page and the Grand Lodge of Virginia, assisted by Fredericksburg Lodge No. 4 where Washington was made a Mason, and the Grand Lodge of Alexandria, of which he was the first Master. Mr. Lawrence Washington was introduced by the President as a lineal descendant of Mary, the Mother of Washington. He gave an interesting sketch of her life, home, parentage, widowhood and the character of her children. The President next introduced the orator of the day, Hon. John W. Daniel. He is said to have pronounced on this occasion the ablest oratorical effort of his life.

Governor O'Ferrall at the request of the Fredericksburg Mary Washington Monument Association read a set of engrossed resolutions which were presented to Mrs. Waite as President of the National Society. This concluded the ceremonies. President Cleveland after holding a general reception on the monument grounds was entertained at the home of Hon. W. Seymour White, editor of the Free Lance, and afterwards Mayor of the city. It was a brilliant gathering, Cabinet Officers and their wives, the Governor of Virginia and Staff, and distinguished citizens of the town and elsewhere to greet them. The ladies of the National Board were entertained at the home of Mrs. V. M. Fleming, president of the local association. President Cleveland repaired to the Mary Washington House where he requested he should receive all the descendants of the Balls and Washingtons. "There he had the satisfaction of grasping the hands and enjoying the conversation of the nearest living relatives of his first and greatest predecessor, in the home of his honored mother."

A banquet was given by the citizens in the Opera House, and a large Ball that night in the same place. Thus closed a memorable day in the annals of Fredericksburg.

Story of Older Monument

The land on which the monument is built, on the same site as that occupied by the first monument, was given by Mr. George Shepherd, a prominent and wealthy merchant, to the Fredericksburg Mary Washington Monument Association, and was transferred at the dedication of the monument by a conditional deed to the National Association.

The first monument to the memory of Mary Washington was partly erected by Silas Burrows of New York, who as rumor has it, fell in love with one of the Gregory girls — great nieces of George Washington. It was of handsome design, but never finished, and the marble shaft lay prostrate for many years, cracked and discolored, while the base, with its beautiful four carved columns was a target for both armies during the Civil war.

The corner stone of this first monument was laid in 1833, with much pomp, the President of the United States —Gen. Andrew Jackson—taking part with Cabinet Officers and escorts, The people of Fredericksburg previous to Mr. Burrows' offer, had made efforts to raise money for a memorial to Mary Washington. Hearing of this he wrote to the Mayor, offering to give and erect the monument himself. The monument had reached completion with the exception of placing the shaft, when Mr. Burrows went abroad and never reappeared, the same Madam Rumor attributing it to the disappointment he experienced at the failure to win the hand of Miss Gregory, the daughter of Mildred Washington, the niece of the immortal George.

The present monument is splendidly cared for by the National Association with the Secretary of the Association, a Fredericksburg lady in charge and living on the grounds in a beautiful cottage built by the National Mary Washington Monument Association.

At the Rising Sun

Where Famous Men Met; and Mine Host Brewed Punch and Sedition.

Standing back a few feet from the Main Street of Fredericksburg, the Rising Sun Tavern looks out on the automobiles and trucks that hurry by over the concrete streets. Silk and woolen mills and "pants" factories spin and weave and rumble, while the old tavern, with the dignity of its century and a half, calmly flaunts the sign of the rising sun with its radii of red light. The knocker that felt the hand of almost every famous American of early days still hangs kindly out.

Built in 1750 or 1760, the Rising Sun Tavern is at least 160 years old. In the days when American men were slowly being forced from their English allegiance it stood in an open space, surrounded by green trees. The road on which it was built ran out from Fredericksburg toward Falmouth and the "upper county," and the tavern was outside the city limits.

If one could stand and see the tavern as in a movie "fade out," the modern houses about it would dim, and, fresh in making and painting, the old tavern would stand alone beside a rutted road alongside which a footpath runs through the grass. Oak trees line the road, and reach down to the river. On the porch, or passing up and down the steps are gentlemen of the Northern Neck, the Potomac plantations, and the Rappahannock Valley, in splendid broadcloth, laced ruffles, black silk stockings, with buckles at the knees and the instep, powdered hair and the short wigs then the fashion, and ladies in the fashionable red cloaks and long, full dresses with the "Gypsy bonnets" tied under their chins, and hair "crimped" and rolled at each side.

At the back yard of the tavern in the old garden grew a profusion of tulips, pink violets, purple iris, hyacinths and the flowering almond and passion fruit, with here and there

When Weedon Was the Host

rose bushes. Inside in the front room flamed the log fire and at the rear of this was the dining-room, where for men and women and boys, the old negro slave who served the gentle folk had mint juleps, or claret that had thrice crossed the ocean, or brandy and soda.

Virginia in the days between 1760 and 1776 reached the "golden age," and it was during these times that George Weedon, host of the Rising Sun, made that hostelry famous for its hospitality, and made himself famous for his constant advocacy of American liberty. Of Weedon, who was later to become a general and win commendation at the Battle of Brandywine, the English traveler, Dr. Smith, wrote: "I put up at the tavern of one Weedon, who was ever active and zealous in blowing the flames of sedition."

Weedon, one of the pioneers of the movement for freedom, made his Tavern the gathering place for all the gentlemen of the "neighborhood" of which Dr. Smith says: "The neighborhood included all of Westmoreland County, the Northern Neck and all other counties as far as Mount Vernon."

John Davis, a Welshman who came to America to teach, has left us a sketch of the tavern of that day and of the people who frequented it, and a part of what Mr. Davis wrote is well worth quoting: "On the porch of the tavern," he says, "I found a party of gentlemen of the neighboring plantations sitting over a bowl of toddy and smoking cigars. On ascending the steps to the piazza, every countenance seemed to say, 'This man has a double claim to our attention, for he is a stranger in the place.' In a moment room was made for me to sit down, and a new bowl of punch called for, and every one addressed me with a smile of conciliation. The higher Virginians seem to venerate themselves. I am persuaded that not one of that company would have felt embarrassed at being admitted to the presence and conversation of the greatest monarch on earth."

Attracted by its hospitality and by the constant meeting before the wood-fire of men whose influence was great, gentlemen from all Virginia came to the Rising Sun. George Mason, who Gillard Hunt of the Library of Congress says was "more than any other man entitled to be called the Father of the Declaration of Independence," was frequently there. The young man from Monticello, Thomas Jefferson, who was Mason's pupil in politics, spent much time at Gunston and was often at the tavern.

George Washington, whose home was in Fredericksburg, knew the tavern well, and Hugh Mercer, a young physician, and brother-in-law of mine host Weedon (they having married the two Misses Gordon), spent a great deal of time there. Other guests who heard the news and who read of events when the weekly stage brought the belated mail from Williamsburg, to the Tavern Postoffice, where "Light Horse" Harry Lee and Charles Lee, from their near-by home at Wakefield, Charles Carter, son of the mighty "King" Carter, who came from "Cleve"; John Marshall, Dr. Mortimer, the Tayloes, of "Mt. Airy"; John Minor, (afterwards general,) of Hazel Hill; young James Monroe, practicing as an attorney in Fredericksburg and acting as a member of the town council and vestryman of St. George's Church; Samuel, Charles and John Augustine Washington, brothers of George, as well as Fielding Lewis, who married George's sister Betty, and was afterwards a general in the revolutionary army. Many of the frequenters of the tavern held high commissions during the war.

It is a matter of undoubted record that these, and half a hundred other young men, whose names were to become synonymous with freedom, discussed at the Rising Sun Tavern the topics of the day, chief among which was the rights of the colonist. The fiery Irishman, George Weedon, arranged and organized conferences and wrote numerous letters, and long before men had ceased to respect the English king, he was bold enough to propose for the first time the toast, "May the Rose grow and the Thistle flourish, and may the Harp be attuned to the cause of American liberty," thus expressing his desire that his native land, and Scotland, should aid America. And he was not disappointed, for afterwards he would say that he was "ever proud that besides himself, America had for generals such Irishmen as 'Mad Anthony' Wayne, Sullivan, Moylan and Irvine."

In these talks at the Rising Sun, where sometimes the great men of the time met night after night, those principles that went in the Bill of Rights of Virginia — were fully discussed before freedom from England was demanded; and here, where gathered lawyers and planters and men of profession, many of them members of the House of Burgesses, there must have been conceived a great many principles that afterwards went to make the Constitution. This was the true "cradle" of American liberty.

John Paul Jones when only thirteen years old, heard the first discussion of such things, probably, when he called at the tavern post-office for mail for his brother, William Paul, who kept a tailor shop and grocery.

When Lord Dunmore seized the powder at Williamsburg in 1775, the first troops organized in Virginia to fight against the authority of the king, started from Fredericksburg. It seems certain that the plans were made at the Rising Sun Tavern, and George Weedon was the leading spirit. Hugh Mercer was elected colonel, Mordecai Buckner, lieutenant-colonel, and Robert Johnson, major. These troops, according to Wirt's Life of Patrick Henry, were stopped by a message from Edmund Randolph, of Williamsburg, saying all was, temporarily, peaceful.

But the apex of the tavern's glory was reached when the great peace ball was held officially to celebrate the end of the war, and Washington led the minuet in the Fredericksburg town hall. Of those who came, tradition says, none failed to visit General Weedon's tavern, though the genial Irishman was now about to leave it and move into the home left without a head when General Mercer fell.

Among those who came to Fredericksburg and were at some time guests at the famous old inn, besides those named

RISING SUN TAVERN
Where the Great Men of Pre-Revolution Days Gathered, and Freedom Was Discussed

Beautiful Colonial Belles

were Brigadier General Stephen Moylan, another Irishman who served as Washington's aide, as commissary general and as commander of troops at Yorktown; Brigadier-General Irvine, Irish too, and here at Weedon's insistence; Count Beaumarchais, author of the "Barber of Seville" and general in the American army; the Marquis de Lafayette, the Viscounts d'Nouvalles, Count d'Estang, Baron Viominel, and many others.

But who were the ladies then? History does not say, but the dancing master, Mr. Christian, who taught the "gentle young ladies" through the "neighborhood," and has left sketches of their personal manner and dress, has described for us a host of them, many of them misses of 15 and 16, who now would be called girls but were quite young ladies then.

Miss Lucy Lightfoot Lee was "tall and stately" (at 16), Mr. Christian says, "wearing a bright chintz gown with a blue stamp, elegantly made, a blue silk quilt, and stays, now said to be the fashion in London but to my mind a great nuisance." While Miss Hale danced in "a white Holland gown, quilt very fine, a lawn apron, her hair crimped up in two rolls at each side and a tuft of ribbon for a cap."

It is easy to surmise that the charming Gregory girls, now married, were there, and that little Maria Mortimer, who on the night following the Peace Ball, at 15 years of age, was hostess for all the great gentlemen, was also a guest, as well as Miss Betsy Lee, Martha Custis, and Posey Custis, Molly Posey, Anne Mason, Alice Lee, and Mary Ambler (later to become the wife of Chief Justice Marshall), Sally Patton, "lately come from England to teach," the two Turberville girls, Priscilla Carter, Jenny Washington and the Lewis girls, the Taylor girls, and the Fitzhughs, of Boscobel and Chatham.

The old tavern is well-preserved and is taken care of by the Association for the Preservation of Virginia Antiquities. Not much change has been made in it since the days of its glory, when at its hospitable hearth young James Monroe

Names of Great Virginians

argued for the emancipation of slaves, George Mason spoke his views on the rights of man, Weedon talked forever "sedition" with Mercer, who hated England since he had felt defeat at the disaster of Colloden and crept from Scotland a hunted man, Jefferson discussed his broad principles, and the Randolphs, Blands, Byrds, Harrisons, Moncures, Taliaferros, Fitzhughs, Lewises of Marmion, Carters of Cleve, Raleigh Travers (of Sir Walter's family) of Stafford, Peter Daniel of "Crows Nest," Thomas Fitzhugh, Selden of Salvington, Brent of Bellevue, Ludwell Lee of "Berry Hill," Richard Henry Lee of "Wakefield," and other famous men gathered, in those crowded days before the Revolution.

Lafayette Comes Back

After Forty Years of Failure, He Hears the Echo of His Youthful Triumph.

Forty years after his return to France at the end of the American Revolution, General Lafayette came back to visit the nation he had helped to create. Cities of the United States heaped honor and hospitality upon him. The people greeted him in villages and taverns as he traveled, and it is not strange that he returned to France "astonished" at the vigor of the young republic.

He himself had seen France taste freedom, turn to the Terror, accept Bonaparte's dictatorship and fight the world — and he had taken his part in it all, even to five years spent in a prison cell. Now he beheld on the throne again the scions of the same monarch who had tried in vain to prevent his aiding America in her fight for freedom, and, his title and estates gone, he must have felt France's failure to realize such ideals of government as he and Washington knew, as keenly as he appreciated the "astonishing" march of democracy on this continent.

Entertained first in the North, Lafayette hurried South to see Jefferson at Monticello for a day. From the Charlottesville estate he traveled to Orange Courthouse, and thence, over the road his army had cut through "The Wilderness" and which even to this day is known as "The Marquis Road," he came to Wilderness Tavern, where he was met by an escort from Fredericksburg.

Fredericksburg was awaiting him, and Lafayette was glad of the opportunity to spend the greater part of a week in the "home town" of George Washington, to visit Washington's relatives, and to meet those of the Revolutionary general still living in the place. He had been to Fredericksburg before in 1774, an honored guest at "The Peace Ball." He had said that he felt more at home in Fredericksburg than anywhere in America.

Peculiar Items of Expense

General Washington, Mrs. Washington, General Mercer, General Weedon — a dozen of his closer friends whom he had left behind forty years ago — were dead, but among the Fredericksburg people there were still numbers who knew him, some who had entertained him, and many who had fought with him.

That Fredericksburg did her best and that good cheer was not lacking when the general arrived, is recorded in the old courthouse of that city in the official bill of expenses for the entertainment of the distinguished guest. On these yellow papers written in the careful hand of that day, are bills for ribbons and laces and cocked hats, sperm candles and cakes, oranges (at $1.20 a dozen), cockades, cloaks and "everything" that might assist in making the November days of the Marquis' stay glide right merrily.

Before the general arrived there was preliminary work, and this is recorded in a number of bills, among them that of Sally Stokes who had one for "cleaning and schowering the town hall, and whitening the steps and cleaning the walls, etc. — I charge for myself and 2 other women — $2.25." Her charge was probably a little high as the work was for the city. "Benj. Day" got the draying contract and profiteered in the following rate:

"Dr. me for myself and team and dray for 4 days hauling for the Entertainment Commit. $6.00." Also among the bills for labor is one:

"To John Scott, Dr. to hire of my man Billy, the painter, for 6 days to paint the market house, $4.50," while "Mary Lucas," a "freewoman," got $1.25 for "sawing 2 1-2 cords of wood."

General Lafayette was met at Orange by a committee and under its escort he journeyed south, (along that forest road which his army cut when with "Mad Anthony Wayne" he followed Tarleton into the unsettled parts of Virginia and the Carolinas,) to the Wilderness and to Fredericksburg. It is possible that some message had to be sent from or to his

George Cary's Great Thirst

escort, in fact it is evident, for George Cary has left record of it, and in presenting his bill he has left as well his individuality and his photograph behind him. If one remembers that brandy was $1.00 a gallon, he needs little more of George Cary's history than this.

"To George Cary for services rendered as messenger, to the Wilderness, including self and horse, $7.00.
"and drink, $1.75"
"Deduct 50c. advanced him by the Mayor, $8.25."

Near Fredericksburg, and almost at the spot where during the Revolution the camp of Hessian prisoners was kept, General Lafayette was met by a military escort commanded by Colonel John Stannard. When the cavalcade reached the city it passed through rows of grown-ups and children and (surely previously rehearsed for many days!), the latter sang in French, "The Marseillaise," and, stepping from his coach, Lafayette marched between the rows of children, singing the anthem of the French revolution.

Only one break was made during the stay of the Marquis in Fredericksburg, if deductions from these old accounts are correct. The town cannon must have "busted." And why it did, and the legitimate enthusiasm which led to such a contretemps, due probably to the exuberance of one who had followed the general in the great war for liberation forty years before, is gathered from these bills:

"To John Phillips, for tending to the gun, $2. Old junk, 37c. Old junk, 27c. Old junk, 23c. 4 kegs of powder, $24., two quarts whisky, 50c."
"To John Phillips, fireing the cannon, $4."
"To Thomas Wright, for 21 panes glass broken by the cannon last Saturday night and on the 19th of November, 10c. a pane and 8x10 each — $2.10."

When General Lafayette left Fredericksburg he went by stage to Potomac Creek, by boat to Washington, by stage to Baltimore, and thence he sailed back to France. With him went Messrs. Mercer and Lewis, both sons of men who had been Generals in the war for Liberty.

Old Court Records

Staid Documents, Writ by Hands That Are Still, Are History For Us.

For simple beauty of line there is probably no Court House in Virginia that equals that at Fredericksburg. While to the casual eye its grace is obvious, to artists' and architects' it makes the stronger appeal, and it is from those familiar with the lines of new and old world buildings that the Court House receive highest praise. Inside, in a modern vault, are many interesting records of the past. The Court House was completed in 1852, at a cost of about $14,000, William M. Boggeth of Baltimore being the contractor, and J. B. Benwick, Jr., of Baltimore, the architect, and its completion marked the end of a thirty years factional fight in the City, which was divided over the issue of building or not building a court house. The decision to build was made by the Council in spite of a petition against such action, signed by one hundred and seventy-two voters.

The second Court House, a small brick building, stood back from the street, on a part of the ground the present structure occupies, and had taken the place of the first plank Court House. But, as early as 1820, the second structure was complained of by the Court, which went so far as to "order" the Council to provide funds for a new structure, to which the Council paid no attention. On June 14, 1849, the Court, composed of Mayor Semple and Justices William H. White and Peter Goolrick, issued an order and appointed a committee, as follows: "Thomas B. Barton, John L. Marye, Robert B. Semple, Wm. C. Beale and John J. Chew, to examine and report to this Court some plan for the enlargement and repairs or rebuilding of the Court House of this Corporation."

But in spite of some excitement following this unusual step of the Court, the Council continued its way undisturbed.

Building a New Courthouse

The Court, however, called before it "the Justices for this Corporation" and at the next session eight Justices — R. B. Semple, Robert Dickey, Beverly R. Welford, William C. Beale, William H. White, Peter Goolrick, William Warren and William Slaughter answered the summons. The report of the committee appointed at the previous session of the Court was made and the Court finally took this action:

"That, in obedience to the act of the General Assembly, which requires that Courts for the Corporations' within this Commonwealth should cause to be erected one good, convenient court house, and it being necessary to build a court house for this corporation," etc., the Court "appoints a commission, consisting of Mayor Semple, Beverly R. Welford, William H. White, Thomas B. Barton and John L. Marye to contract for a court house."

But, despite this, and because of the divided sentiment of the people and the inaction of the Council, the Court did not build a court house, and at a later meeting voted four to four on a motion to rescind their previous order. After various moves and counter moves, the issue was carried into a regular election held in March, 1851, and a Council in favor of a new Court House was chosen. The erection of the present structure in 1852 ended a thirty years disagreement, which built up bitter factions in the town and left animosities, which did not subside until the Civil War came on. For many years, until the new Fire House was built, the old hand-drawn fire apparatus was housed in the south wing of the building.

The bell which is now in the tower of the Court House, formerly hung in the second court house, and sounded the call to public meetings, as it does today, and the alarms of fire and war. It was presented to the town by Silas Wood in 1828, and has his name and that date on it, as well as the name of the maker, "Revere, Boston."

From the earliest times, debtors who could not pay their bills were imprisoned in the jail in Court House square or, more properly, slept in the jail and were imprisoned in the square; for they were allowed the freedom of the whole square and the adjacent streets, but were not allowed to enter any store or building on the opposite sides of the streets. Many men of prominence, it is said, spent short periods in this "Debtors' Prison," awaiting the time when their release could be secured under the "Poor Debtors' Law," which gave them freedom when by a schedule of their property they proved they had no means to meet their obligations. In 1840, the Court extended the bounds of the "Debtors' Prison" to include four blocks in the center of the city, and the "footways adjoining them"; but to go beyond these bounds was contempt of Court.

No existing records establish what Courts held session in Fredericksburg prior to the Revolution, and it is probable that successors of Mayor Lawrence Smith were empowered as Governors and Judges until 1727, after which time the Trustees of the town may have chosen magistrates, or the colonial Governors may have done this.

It is established that the first Court in Fredericksburg was created by the General Assembly in 1781, when Fredericksburg was incorporated and given a Common Council and a Hustings Court. The first session of this Hustings Court was held April 15, 1782, with the following Justices present: Charles Mortimer, William McWilliams, James Somerville, Charles Dick, Samuel Ruddy, and John Julien, "the same being Mayor, Recorder and Aldermen of the town." This continued the only Court until 1788, when nineteen District Courts were established in the State by the General Assembly, and one of them was located at Fredericksburg. These courts were presided over by two of the ten Judges of the General Court at Richmond. Among the many men of prominence who appeared before this District Court were James Monroe, Edmund Randolph, and Francis Brooke. This District Court was abolished in 1809 and a Circuit Court took its place. This new court was now presided over by *one* of the Judges of the General Court at Richmond. With some changes these courts continue to the present, but are presided over by specially chosen Circuit Judges. But the Circuit Court is not held at Fredericksburg.

The Hustings Court, meanwhile, was the local court for Fredericksburg until 1870, when it became the "Corporation Court" over which, instead of three Justices of the Peace, the Assembly now provided there be a Judge "who shall be learned in law." Judge John M. Herndon was the first Judge of this Court, in 1870, and was succeeded by Judge John T. Goolrick, 1877, Judge Montgomery Slaughter followed him, Judge A. Wellington Wallace presided for some years, and Judge Embry served until Judge John T. Goolrick was again chosen Judge and has continued on the bench for the last 16 years.

A more remarkable record is that of the men of the Chew family, who for ninety-nine years and eleven days were the Clerks of this Court, succeeding each other by appointment and election in direct lineal line. Henry Armistead, first Clerk of the Court, died August 1, 1787, and on August 6, 1787, John Chew, Jr., was appointed to the vacancy. In 1806 his son, Robert S. Chew, succeeded; In 1826 the latter's son John J. Chew succeeded; In 1867, the latter's son, Robert S. Chew succeeded and held office until his death in 1886. Mr. J. Willard Adams is now Clerk of the Corporation Court.

There are many interesting documents in the vaults of the Court House, many of them mere scraps, as that which tells of an inquest in 1813 over the "Body of a sailor from the Frigate 'Constitution,'" who was drowned here in the river, and which indicates that the famed old boat was once at Fredericksburg Wharf.

Among the oldest and most interesting documents in the archives of the Court House, is a "List of Males Capable of Militia Duty — 1785." and of the two hundred and sixty-five then listed, (which would indicate a population of about 1,300 in the city at that time). There are few names now known in Fredericksburg, nevertheless, there are some, and of these familiar names the following are examples:

Mary Washington's Will

"Dr. Mortimer, Dr. Brooke, Dr. French, Dr. Hall, Dr. Gillis, Dr. Hand" and "Bradford, Taylor, Yates, Walker, Maury, Minor, Herndon, White, Brent, Johnson, Wheeler, Gray, Jenkins, Allen, Crutchfield, Ferneyhough, Brown, Chew, Weedon, Colbert, Washington, Brooks, Ingram, Middleton, Spooner, Payne, Gordon, Young, Thompson, Berry, Slaughter, Lewis, Clarke," and many others whose descendants are well known in this city and vicinity.

The will of Mary Washington, written by James Mercer, an attorney who was also Chief Justice of the General Court, (the highest court of Virginia) and signed by Mary Washington, is preserved in the Court House and has been seen by hundred of callers. The will was made May 20, 1788, and was filed after the death of Mrs. Washington.

"In the name of God, Amen. I, Mary Washington, of Fredericksburg, in the County of Spottsylvania, being in good health, but calling to mind the uncertainty of this life and willing to dispose of what remains of my earthly estate, do make and publish this, my last will, recommending my soul into the hands of my Creator, hoping for a remission of all my sins through the merits and mediation of Jesus Christ, the Saviour of Mankind. I dispose of all my worldly estate as follows:

Imprimis: I give to my son, General George Washington, all my lands on Accokeek Run, in the County of Stafford, and also my negro boy, George, to him and his Heirs forever; also my best bed, bedstead and Virginia cloth curtains, (the same that stands in my best room), my quilted Blue and White quilt and my best dressing glass.

Item: I give and devise to my son, Charles Washington, my negro man Tom, to him and his assigns forever.

Item: I give and devise to my daughter, Betty Lewis, my phaeton and my bay horse.

Item: I give and devise to my daughter-in-law, Hannah Washington, my purple cloth cloak lined with shay.

MARY WASHINGTON'S HOME
In the Garden Mrs. Washington Greeted Young Lafayette. She Lived And Died Here

Mary Washington's Will

Item: I give and bequeath to my grandson, Corbin Washington, my negro wench, Old Bet, my riding chair and two black horses, to him and his assigns forever.

Item: I give and bequeath to my grandson, Fielding Lewis, my negro man, Frederick, to him and his assigns forever; also, eight silver table spoons, half of my crockery ware, and the blue and white Tea China, with book case, oval table, one bedstead, two table cloths, six red leather chairs, half my pewter, and one-half my iron kitchen furniture.

Item: I give and bequeath to my granddaughter, Betty Carter, my negro woman, Little Bet, and her future increase, to her and her assigns forever; also my largest looking glass, my walnut writing desk with drawers, a square dining table, one bed, bedstead, bolster, one pillow, one blanket and pair of sheets, white Virginia cloth counterpane, and purple curtains, my red and white china, teaspoons and other half of my pewter, crockery ware, and the remainder of my iron kitchen furniture.

Item: I give to my grandson, George Washington, my next best dressing glass, one bed, bedstead, bolster, one pillow, one pair of sheets, one blanket and counterpane.

Item: I devise all my wearing apparel to be equally divided between my granddaughters, Betty Carter, Fanny Ball and Milly Washington; but should my daughter, Betty Lewis, fancy any one, two or three articles, she is to have them before a division thereof.

Lastly: I nominate and appoint my said son, General George Washington, executor of this, my Will, and as I owe few or no debts, I desire my Executor to give no security nor to appraise my estate, but desire the same may be allotted to my devisees with as little trouble and delay as may be, desiring their acceptance thereof as all the token I now have to give them of my love for them.

In Witness Whereof, I have hereunto set my hand and seal this 20th day of May, 1788.

Mary Washington.

Witness: John Ferneyhough.

Burial in Streets Stopped

Signed, sealed and published in our presence, and signed by us in the presence of the said Mary Washington, and at her desire.

J. Mercer
Joseph Walker."

Among the orders of the Court, found on the Order Books, are some which are of interest as bearing on old customs of the town. One of the first of these was entered March 1, 1784, when the Court "proceeded to settle the allowances to the officers of the Corporation" as follows: "Mr. John Minor, Jr., Attorney for the Commonwealth, two thousand pounds tobacco; Mr. Henry Armistead, Clerk, twelve hundred pounds tobacco; John Legg, Sergeant, twelve hundred pounds tobacco; Henry Armistead, for attending all Courts of inquiry, four hundred pounds; sergeant for same, five hundred and seventy pounds; Wm. Jenkins, goaler, three hundred and sixty-four pounds."

February 7, 1785, "Robert Brooke" (afterwards Governor of Virginia in 1794-96, and still later Attorney General) and Bushrod Washington, (Uncle of George Washington and later Chief Justice of the Supreme Court) were admitted to practice law.

April 25, 1801, the first "watchman" (policeman) was appointed for the town.

In a peculiar report, made March 27, 1802, the Grand Jury took steps to put a stop to "a nuisance, the numerous obstructions in the streets, particularly in St. George Street lot; burying the dead in George and Princess Anne Streets; also the irregular burying in the ground west of and adjoining Prince Edward." These graves, the report shows, were on George, Princess Anne, and in Hanover Street, west of Princess Anne, and on George Street between Main and the river.

After twenty-two years, the Court issued its first authorization for a Minister of the Gospel (none but the Church of

England ceremony was before recognized) to perform the marriage ceremony, December 24, 1804, to "Benj. Essex," Methodist. Others followed in this order: Samuel Wilson, Presbyterian, September 22, 1806; William James, Baptist, June 13, 1811.

The undisputed fact that John Forsythe, who was in his generation one of America's most famous men, and a sketch of whose life is given elsewhere, was born in Fredericksburg, is contained in this entry, dated January 12, 1832.

"The Court orders it to be certified that it was proved to their satisfaction, by the evidence of Francis S. Scott, a witness sworn in Court, that Major Robert Forsythe of the Revolutionary army, had two children, one of whom, Robert, died under age and unmarried, and the other, John, is now alive, being a Senator in Congress from Georgia."

Among the Court's first acts after establishment, the Hustings Court, on May 20, 1782, thus fixed the prices of certain commodities in the "Taverns": "Good West India Rum, one pound per gallon; bread, ten shillings; whiskey, six; strong beer, four; good West India rum toddy, ten shillings; brandy toddy, seven shillings six pence; rum punch, fifteen shillings; brandy punch, twelve; rum grog, six; brandy grog, five. Diet: one meal, one shilling six pence; lodging, one shilling and three pence; 'stablidge' and hay, two shillings; oats and corn, nine pence per gallon."

The prices of intoxicants is hard to explain. Rum is at the rate of $5.00 per gallon, but apparently whiskey is only $1.25. A later ordinance of prices, made May 10, makes various changes.

"Breakfast, fifty cents; dinner, fifty; supper, fifty; lodging, twenty-five; grain, per gallon, twelve and one-half; stablidge and hay per night, twenty-five; Madera Wine, per quart, one dollar; Champagne, per quart, one dollar and fifty cents; other wine, per quart, fifty cents; French brandy, twelve and one-half cents per gill; Rum, twelve and one-half cents per gill; Gin, twelve and one-half cents per gill."

Some of the Judges

A pure judiciary is one of the best assurances of good government, and Virginia is proud of her Judges, who on the average, have been and are men of learning, and acknowledged ability.

In this book, we can only chronicle briefly the names of some who have presided in the Circuit Courts of this circuit.

First is the name of John Tayloe Lomax, who had occupied a chair in the law school at the University of Virginia, and who had written several books treating on law, before he came to preside as judge here.

Richard Coleman, of the distinguished family of that name from Caroline County;

Eustace Conway, one of the very youngest men elected by the people, and who died in a few months after he had assumed the duties;

John Critcher, who soon resigned the judicial office to become an officer in the Confederate Army;

William Stone Barton, who was a splendid Judge, a fearless soldier and a Christian;

John E. Mason, who executed all the duties of his high office intelligently and conscientiously.

Echoes of the Past

"Ghosts of Dead Hours, and Days That Once Were Fair"

Fredericksburg was, in anti-bellum days, the center of a large number of slave holding land proprietors who lived within its gates, yet cultivated their farms in the adjacent territory, hence the colored population of the town was large; and very much to the credit of these colored people as well as a testimonial to the manner of their treatment, and to the methods of their humane and kind discipline, the colored population was law abiding and polite. They were religious in their tendencies, and church going in their practices. For several years they worshipped in a church of their own situated on the banks of the Rappahannock known as Shiloh Baptist Church — for in this section they were Baptist in their creed. After the war, in consequence of some feuds and factions, they divided up into several churches, all of the Baptist denomination. Clinging to the name, there is now "Shiloh Old Site" — and "Shiloh New Site" and some mild rivalry.

Among the old time colored brethren were some unique characters. We note a few only: Scipio, or as he called himself, Scipio Africanus from Ethiopia, was very popular; kindly and charitable in disposition he was probably the only infidel among that race. One afternoon, at a Baptizing which always took place in the River, a very fat sister came near being drowned. Aftet she was immersed by the preacher, gasping and struggling, she came up and Scip becoming excited yelled to the colored divine — "Stop there Brother! Stop I tell you! If you douse that gal again some white man goin' to lose a valuable nigger by this here foolishness!" Needless to say the indignant divine released the sister and turned his wrath on Scipio.

About the Colored People

Another colored character was Edmund Walker, who kept a coffee house. He openly proclaimed he wanted no "poor white trash." Over his emporium in big letters flourished this sign — "walk in gentlemen, sit at your ease, Pay for what you call for, and call for what you please."

Jim Williams was known as a good cook, as well as huntsman. His Master, Col. Taliaferro told Jim one day that he expected great men for dinner some time soon, and, "Jim, I want a turkey, a fat turkey fattened in a coop, not shot Jim!" When the day came and dinner was served, Col. Taliaferro's knife in carving, struck a shot or two. Infuriated, the old Colonel yelled at Jim — "Didn't I tell you not to bring me any turkey with a shot in it?" Jim who had obtained the turkey after dark replied, "Dem shots was 'tended for me not for the turkey. The white folks shot at me, but the turkey got the shot."

The loyalty of the colored men and women for their old Masters and Mistresses during the war cannot be commended too highly. Told time and again that a victory for the Federal soldiers meant their freedom, many of them refused to leave their old homes, and remained steadfast to the end. While we cannot enumerate many of these, the opportunity to chronicle the name of one, still living cannot be overlooked. The Rev. Cornelius Lucas, who in the dark and dreadful days of war, followed his old owners, the Pollocks, is with us yet. He was with them on the march and in camp, waited on them, and ministered to them. One of the Chapters of the Daughters of the Confederacy in this town, recently decorated him with its testimonial, its cross of honor.

We know of no locality situated so near the Mason and Dixon line as is Fredericksburg where the Union Armies came with their propaganda of freedom for the slaves, which presents more of the love of the former slaves for their former Masters, and more obedience to law and order than is the case with the colored people of the town of Fredericksburg, for with rare exceptions, there has been no flagrant violation of the laws. We are of the opinion that this book would not indeed respond to the requirements of endeavoring to sketch the town and its life, without embodying within its pages what it includes of the colored men and women whose lives have been spent within its limits.

Early in the nineteenth century, on May 7th, 1833, Fredericksburg was visited by President Andrew Jackson and escort, the occasion, one of the most important of that period, being the laying of the corner stone of the old Mary Washington Monument. People from all over this general section gathered to greet the hero of New Orleans, and in addition to the detachment of Marines, which was the President's honor guard, military organizations from Washington, Alexandria, Fauquier County and Fredericksburg, led by Col. John Bankhead, chief marshal, took part in the large parade that preceded the ceremonies.

History has recorded for us correctly what took place on the occasion. The President spoke as did also other distinguished men and, as in those remote days orators were not sparing with the time they took, undoubtedly the long suffering people stood a verbal fusilage that lasted hours. But in the end they were repaid, for the program was followed by feasting and drinking and a general merry time, at which wines, liquors and barbacued beef were served to 5,000 people, under a big tent.

The main reception was held in the old Wallace house, which formerly stood on the site now occupied by the Baker and Wallace wholesale drygoods house, and it was the scene of an incident that convulsed the dignified gathering, which was hard put to control its laughter. It came about as follows.

While traveling by road from Quantico (which was reached by boat from Washington,) to Fredericksburg, the presidential party encountered a Major Randolph, of the army, who lately had been court martialed and reprimanded on a charge that now is unknown. Major Randolph had appealed the decision of the court to the President, who much to the indignation of the Major, approved the findings. When

General Lee's Week's Visit

Major Randolph met the President, he stopped, saluted and then questioned him regarding his decision. The President's replies were not satisfactory to the indignant major and he pulled the nose of the Hero of New Orleans. News of the occurrence quickly got about the town.

That night a certain old gentleman of the most generous hospitality and the kindest of hearts but with very poor social instincts, was introduced to the President. His mental processes are not known, naturally, but probably in a desire to be especially gracious and to show that Fredericksburg and its people were deeply considerate of the welfare of their President, and concerned in all that happened to him, the old gentleman grasped the hand of the chief dignitary of the land, bowed very low and said, "Mr. President, I am indeed very glad to meet you and I sincerely hope, Sir, that Major Randolph did not hurt you when he pulled your nose to-day."

The President flared up momentarily but seeing the innocence written in the countenance of the old gentleman, and the convulsions of those around him, he joined heartily in the laughter and assured his questioner that he was quite unharmed.

In 1869 the Episcopal Council of the State gathered in St. George's Church and to this Council as a delegate from Grace Church, Lexington, of which he was a vestryman, came General Robert E. Lee the beloved hero of the South. Just across the street from St. George's Church was the home of Judge William S. Barton and there he was the honored guest. Coming so shortly after the close of the war when the people were in almost a frenzy of sympathy for him and sorrow for their "Lost Cause" he produced an impression that will never be forgotten by those who saw him.

The Barton house was besieged by young and old, anxious to shake hands with him. The Bartons gave a large reception, and the writer recalls that scene as if it were yesterday.

MONUMENT TO MERCER
*Erected by Congress to the Brilliant General Who Fell at Princeton.
The Street Is Washington Avenue*

General Lee's Week's Visit

General Lee stood with Judge Barton and his stately wife; General Barton and his wife, and the peerless beauty, Mary Triplett, who was the niece of the Bartons. To describe General Lee would be superfluous. The majesty of his presence has been referred to. He inspired no awe or fear, but a feeling of admiration as if for a superior being. People who spoke to him turned away with a look of happiness, as if some long felt wish had been gratified. Toward the conclusion of the reception, when only a few intimate friends remained, some of the young girls ventured to ask for a kiss, which was given in fatherly fashion. The Council lasted a week, from Sunday to Sunday and for that time General Lee remained at the Bartons.

The home life of this truly representative Virginia family brings back elusive dreams of the charmed days of old when a gentle elegance, a dignity, a grace of welcome that was unsurpassed in any land, made them ideal as homes and supreme in hospitality, and nowhere was this more clearly evidenced than in the family of Judge Barton. General Lee was serenaded here by Prof. A. B. Bowering's Band, the same Band which accompanied the gallant 30th Virginia Regiment on its marches, and cheered them in Camp with patriotic airs.

It was Bowering's Band that, when the body of Stonewall Jackson was removed from the Capitol in Richmond to the railway station, played the Funeral Dirge. Prof. Bowering has led other bands since then, and is at present the conductor of an excellent one.

It was at about this time that Father Ryan wrote one of his most beautiful poems, of which this is the last verse:

> "Forth from its scabbard, all in vain,
> Bright flashed the sword of Lee;
> 'Tis shrouded now in its sheath again,
> It sleeps the sleep of our noble slain
> Defeated, yet without a stain,
> Proudly and peacefully."

Mayors of Fredericksburg

The following is a chronological list of mayors of Fredericksburg with the number of years served by each: Dr. Charles Mortimer, 3; William McWilliams, 1; James Somerville, 3; George Weedon, 1; George French, 8; Benjamin Day, 2; William Harvey, 2 and less than a month of the third year, when he died in office; Fontaine Maury, 3; William Taylor, 1; David C. Ker, 2; William S. Stone, 1; Charles L. Carter, 1 year and six months, resigning when half his first term was out; William Smock, six months, serving the unexpired half of Charles L. Carter's first term; Richard Johnston, 1; Joseph Walker, 1; John Scott, 1; Garret Minor, 2; Robert Mackay, 2; David Briggs, 1.

Briggs' term ended in March, 1821. Up to this time no mayor had served more than 1 year consecutively, but after this date several served for many years following each other. Following Briggs was Robert Lewis, who died in office after nearly nine years; Thomas Goodwin, died in office after nearly seven years; John H. Wallace, 2; Benjamin Clarke 6; Robert Baylor Semple, died in office after nearly nine years; John L. Marye, Jr., 1; Peter Goolrick, 3 years and one month, resigning just after the beginning of his fourth term and almost immediately before the Civil War; John S. Cardwell, 2; William S. Scott, 1; Montgomery Slaughter, the War Mayor, who succeeded Peter Goolrick, (when the latter resigned because the council had refused to endorse some of his appointments), and served until removed by the military authorities after a few days more than eight years. He was succeeded by Charles E. Mallam, appointed by the military authorities in April, 1868, and removed by them in just a little more than a year. William E. Nye, who followed, was appointed by the military but resigned in less than a year. He was succeeded by Lawrence B. Rose, elected by the council and twice later by the people, serving altogether 5 years, two months and twenty days, dying during his last term; William Roy Mason, resigning after serving twenty-seven days of his first term, to which he was elected by the people. Robert Banks Berrey, 2;

Building of the Railroad

Hugh S. Doggett, 3; Joseph W. Sener, 4; Josiah Hazard, 4; Absalom Rowe, 9 years and eleven months, dying in office during his last term; W. Seymore White, 1 year and not quite five months, dying in office; Henry R. Gouldman, seven months; Marion G. Willis, 6 years; Thomas P. Wallace, 4; H. Lewis Wallace, 4; Josiah P. Rowe, a son of Absalom Rowe, 8; J. Garnett King is at present serving.

So far as can be gathered ex-Mayor J. P. Rowe is the only son of a mayor who ever held the same office which his father had filled before him.

The Richmond, Fredericksburg and Potomac Railroad, the great Trunk Line between the North and the South, in 1837 completed its line to Fredericksburg by rail, a stage line thence to Potomac Creek, and steamer connection was made from here to Washington. In 1842, on the 18th of November, the line was completed to Aquia Creek, making it a total of 75 miles in length. In 1860 Peter V. Daniel was elected president, and during his administration the road was fearfully damaged by the Civil War. In 1865, the company, after much rebuilding, again opened service to Aquia Creek. In 1872 the line was extended to Quantico, and connecting there with the Washington-Quantico road, filled in the missing link of railway from the North to the South.

The railroad has always been financially successful and has provided a service of exceptional convenience. It has the remarkable record of never having killed a passenger within its cars, and but two from any cause whatever. Under the Hon. Eppa Hunton it operates now with great efficiency and over its tracks pass a string of trains during all of the twenty-four hours. On all of its trains an employee calls attention just before passing the house where Stonewall Jackson died. The house has been purchased and preserved to posterity by the railroad—an act for which it deserves the highest commendation, as it does for the monument it gen-

Jefferson Davis' Speech

erously built at Hamilton's Crossing, where heavy fighting occurred during the battle of Fredericksburg.

Jefferson Davis, when a member of the Senate, was loath to leave that body and opposed breaking up of the Union. But, when his own State of Mississippi called, he answered. He had been educated at West Point and had fought in Mexico. When the representatives met at Montgomery, Alabama, and elected him President of the Confederacy, he accepted. When the seat of government was moved to Richmond, he, of course, came with it.

Soon after this he paid Fredericksburg a visit and while in the town was a guest of Temple Doswell, Esq., at his home on the corner of Princess Anne and Lewis Streets. As soon as it was known that he was here a band, accompanied by a multitude of citizens and Confederate soldiers, gave him a complimentary reception, to which he replied, in a brief address, from the porch. The writer remembers very clearly how he appeared. He was tall, thin, beardless, slightly bald, dressed in black broad cloth that was slightly worn looking.

Mr. Davis came to review the troops stationed on the Potomac at Acquia, as well as some encamped at Fredericksburg. He expressed himself as very much pleased, not only with the hospitable reception accorded him, but also, with the conditions of the troops and the general management of the situation then under General Daniel Ruggles.

It is an unusual coincidence that during the war between the States, Fredericksburg should have had within its gates, President Lincoln of the United States and President Jefferson Davis of the Confederate States, and that each made a public address from places three blocks apart.

This National Cemetery is located on one of the most prominent and imposing hills overlooking the City of Fredericksburg, formerly called Willis Hill. On July 15, 1865, this location was selected and the cemetery begun. It has since been made beautiful with shrubbery and flowers and terraced,

The National Cemetery

and now it is known for its attractive appearance. It is, in fact, counted as one of the most beautiful cemeteries in this Country. It comprises about twelve acres. Of the soldiers gathered from the adjacent battlefields there are of the known dead 2,496 and of the unknown 12,798.

Very many handsome monuments are erected on these grounds, among them one by General Butterfield in memory of the 5th Corps; another to General Humphreys by the State of Pennsylvania; and by the same State a monument in memory of the 127th Pennsylvania Volunteers. Head stones mark the resting place of very many others.

On each recurring Decoration Day, May 30th, from a beautifully constructed forum, services are held in tribute to the memory of the brave men who sleep there. At these services many who wore the grey and fought on the other side unite with the boys who wore the blue, in paying this tribute.

Near Fredericksburg Governor Spottswood instituted the first iron work in America, and an old plate cast in his furnace is now in the possession of Mr. Val Dannehl of this city. It is probably the oldest piece of cast iron in America.

Governor Spottswood built the village of Germanna on he upper river for German workmen brought over here, and it was from that place, the first Courthouse of Spotsylvania County, that the Knights of the Golden Horseshoe began their journey. The mansion of this famous Virginian stood close beside the Germanna road.

Today, almost on that spot, stands a small white cottage, and within it are various relics of the Old Governor and his family and of the battle of the Wilderness.

But the strangest thing about the small cottage is that within it lives, with his wife, Alexander Spottswood, the lineal descendant of the Governor. Mr. Spottswood stands over six feet, erect and with the bearing that inevitably proclaims the descendants of great men. His daughter recently married Mr. E. H. Willis.

Patti Once Lived Here

    Thus a Spottswood lives today on the tract where the great Virginia Governor built his mansion and where he founded the famous Spottswood mines and furnace almost two hundred years ago.

    An incident brought the great singer Patti to Fredericksburg, to remain for some time. When she was a girl of sixteen, just beginning to train for her great career in Grand Opera, her brother Carlo Patti expected to institute a school of music and was here for that purpose when he was taken suddenly ill. She came with her sister Madam Strackosh to see her brother. He remained ill for months and his sisters were with him during the entire time. They boarded at the Old Exchange Hotel on Main Street, now the Hotel Maury, and gave more than one concert at what was known then as "The Citizens Hall." If there are few here now who remember her, there is still among us one woman, a little child at the time, whom the singer often held in her arms and caressed. The parents of the child were boarding at the Hotel temporarily and the mother and Adelina became great friends and remained so for many years. Madam Strackosh and her famous sister said they enjoyed "real life" in our little Southern town. Carlo after regaining his health went farther South, joined a Confederate Company, and again as one of the boys in gray under the stars and bars, was in Fredericksburg and was well known to the writer. He entertained the weary boys in camp when the hard days were over, with his beautiful songs.

    John Forsythe referred to in the above order was born in 1781 in a frame house, now standing at the corner of Prince Edward and Fauquier Streets. He graduated from the Princeton Academy early in life, moving later with his family to Georgia where he studied law, practiced and in 1808 he was elected Attorney General, and in 1812 was chosen Congressman and served until 1818.

    In 1819 he was appointed Minister to Spain and while acting as Minister, he was instrumental in the ratification of

NATIONAL CEMETERY
And Monument to the Fifth Corps. Here Sleep Thousands Who Died in the Battles About Fredericksburg

the treaty with the Country for the cession of Florida to the United States.

In 1827 he was elected Governor of Georgia and in 1829 became a member of the Senate and was in that body when he accepted the office of Secretary of State, which position he occupied to the end of Van Buren's administration. He died in the City of Washington, October 21, 1841, and is buried in the Congressional Cemetery.

Fighting "Joe" Hooker, as his troops called him and as he was, came here shortly after the war to gather evidence to refute the charges his enemies at the North were disseminating against him in a campaign of scandal. He attempted while here, and he was here for a long period, to show that his failure was not entirely his own fault, and the evidence which he procured , together with his own statements proved sufficiently that Gen. Hooker's plan for the campaign at Chancellorsville far surpassed any conception of any other Northern general. They left the inference also (Lincoln had warned him in a letter that his insubordination to Burnside and other superior officers would one day result in his inferiors failing to co-operate with him), that Sedgwick had not put his full heart into the battle, for, important factor in the movement that he was, he started one day late and allowed 4,000 men at Salem Church to hold back the advance of his 30,000 men. Had he won this fight, he could have been at Chancellorsville and turned the tide of battle long before Jackson's genius had ruined Hooker's army.

The subject of this sketch, Judge James B. Sener, was the son of Captain and Mrs. Joseph W. Sener. His father was several times Mayor of this city. He graduated when quite a young man, with the degree of Bachelor of Law, from the University of Virginia, and was a very successful practitioner for many years in the courts of this State. He was elected to represent the first Virginia district in the Congress of the

Abraham Lincoln's Address

United States several years after the civil war. After his retirement from Congress he was appointed by President Hayes Chief Justice of the then Territory of Wyoming. After performing the duties of this office very acceptably for several years he returned to Virginia, and again took up the practice of his profession. Much of his time was spent in Washington where he died. He was buried in Fredericksburg with Masonic honors, being a very active member of Lodge No. 4, A. F. and A. M. of this city.

When the Federal army first held Fredericksburg, during the winter of 1861, President Lincoln came to stay at Chatham and hold a grand review of the army of the Potomac. He was accompanied by Wm. H. Seward, Secretary of State, and Edward Staunton, Secretary of War. On the plateau behind Chatham there was held a great artillery review. On the following day the President, accompanied by some of his cabinet officers and the staff officers of the army, crossed the river on the lower pontoon bridge. They rode immediately to the provost marshal's headquarters in the building on the corner of Princess Anne and George Streets, which the National Bank now occupies. After taking lunch with General Patrick and in response to the calls of some troops present, President Lincoln from the front steps made a short but splendid address. The writer of this, sat on the steps of the St. George's Church, on the opposite side of the street and heard President Lincoln's speech.

On the Bowling Green road, a mile from town, a stone marked "Stuart-Pelham" shows about where those two brilliant young men met when they advanced their guns against the Northern host. In the woods, back of Fredericksburg, a stone marks General Lee's winter headquarters — where stood his tents. The spot where Cobb fell is marked, and there is a marker where the pontoon landed near the foot of Hawk street. The New Jersey monuments are near Salem Church,

Other Distinguished Visitors

General Hays monument (where he was killed) near Plank road on the Brock road. "Lee to the Rear" one mile west of Brock on Plank road, Sedgwick's monument near Spotsylvania Court House. Where Jackson fell, monument two miles west of Chancellorsville on Plank Road. "Lee's Headquarters," marker, Spotsylvania Court House. Lee and Jackson's Last Meeting, near Leavell's..

In the midst of the war England sent Lord Wolesley, who became the Commander-in-Chief of the English Army, to serve a short time as Military Observer with the army of General Lee. He was with General Lee about Fredericksburg and in his commentaries on him said, "There was about General Lee an air of fine nobility, which I have never encountered in any other man I have met." General Wolesley attended a dance here in the house then called the Alsop house, on Princess Anne Street, now occupied by the Shepherds.

The Prince of Wales, who afterwards became King Edward the Seventh, visited Fredericksburg in 1859. The Prince was accompanied by the Duke of New Castle, Lord Lyons and others of the Royal family. They were welcomed here in an address by the late Maj. Elliott M. Braxton. The local band played "God save the Queen" and flowers and bouquets were presented to the Prince.

Among those who came in time of peace we record the name of one whose fame is known to all English readers. Thackeray, the great English novelist, was here, and on taking leave said, "To come to Virginia and mingle with its people, to learn how they live and see their home life, is to have England pictured to you again."

It was perfectly natural that Chester A. Arthur should be often a visitor to Fredericksburg for he married Miss Ellen Lewis Herndon, of this city, a daughter of Captain W. L. Herndon, whose distinguished life has been touched upon. The home in which President Arthur stopped on his visit is on Main Street, now occupied by Mrs. R. B. Buffington.

Other Distinguished Visitors

Certainly the greatest orator who ever visited Fredericksburg was Edward Everett, of Massachusetts, distinguished among literary men of his day. He came to this city to speak and was entertained in several homes here. He afterwards spoke all over the Nation in an effort to aid the Mount Vernon Association to purchase Washington's home.

An English officer Colonel Henderson, whose life of "Stonewall Jackson" is from a literary and military standpoint the best work of its nature in the world, came here and stayed for a long period securing data for his book. He lived during his time here at the Old Eagle Hotel, now the Hotel Maury.

Among our old time merchants was Mr. William Allen. His son married and lived in many foreign lands. The son's wife died and he returned to visit his father bringing his beautiful little daughter, a child of ten or eleven years. The writer recalls her at that time, with her lovely golden curls.

Again the father left, and we next hear of the little girl as Madam Romero, wife of the once Secretary of State of Mexico and then Ambassador to the United States from Mexico. During the stay of Ambassador Romero at Washington, this girl of Virginia lineage became the leader of the social life of the Capitol of our Nation, and one of the most popular women ever known there.

Another nobleman who came here drawn by the quaintness of the old American town and his desire to see the home of Washington, was the Count De Paris, of the French Royal Family.

The Irish poet, Thomas Moore, was here once and declared he would not leave America until he had been a guest in an old Virginia home.

Where Beauty Blends

Old Gardens, at Old Mansions, Where Bloom Flowers from Long Ago

Buds and blossoms everywhere! and honey-bees, butterflies and birds! It is Spring now in the lush meadows and sweeping hills about Fredericksburg. Flowers, leaves, shrubs and vines have burst forth once more with joy and life. The wild tangle of beauty and fragrance is everywhere perceptible; hedges of honeysuckle, whose hidden foundation is the crumbling old stone wall, trellises heavy with old-time roses, arbors redolent with sweet grapevine, sturdy oaks and maples, whose branches shelter the clinging tendrils and the purple wistaria blossoms, borders, gay with old-time favorites, heliotrope, portulaca, petunias, verbenas and hollyhocks, and the loved English ivy, with a welcome right of way wherever its fancy leads.

The characteristic which is conceded to be the chief charm of Fredericksburg is its historic association and its picturesque past. This feature alone does not appeal to all who agree that the old town is charming, but when this is combined with romantic and interesting tales of the gentry of years agone who have won immortality not only in this locality, but in this world, the charm is undeniably irresistible to all. Fredericksburg has many beauty spots which combine these conditions — spots which are of increasing pride to residents and visitors.

Some of the gardens here are old, very old, antedating by many years the celebrated formal gardens at Mt. Vernon, but few preserve so well their pristine form. Though the box-bordered parterres have largely disappeared, the old-time favorites are here still, the same loved shrubbery "just grown tall," descended from those set out originally by those of

Mary Washington's Home

generations gone. Mazie V. Caruthers has, in a few words, unknowingly delineated some of the garden spots here:

> "Long, brick-paved paths, beside which row on row,
> Madonna lilies in their sweetness grow —
> Planted by hands to dust turned long ago;
>
> Odors of fern and moss and pine are there —
> Wild loveliness of roses everywhere
> With pinks and mignonette their fragrance share;
>
> Around the dial, stained by sun and showers
> (Whose slender finger marks the passing hours),
> Stand purple iris, proudest of the flowers;"

At the corner of Charles and Lewis Streets stands the pretty little garden spot, which, since the year 1775 has been associated with Mary Washington. The tall and vigorous, pungent and aromatic box-wood trees, planted by her own hand, seem typical today of the splendid old lady. A small section of the pathway bordered by the same old shrub, which led to "Betty's" home at Kenmore, is still here And here is also the sweet-scented lavender, and the roses, and near the high board fence on the north, is the sun dial, that still and silent informant of the passing hours. Washington, Mason, Jefferson, Marshall, the Lees — a score of the great have trod these shaded walks.

Not far away are two frame structures. The style of each bears the unmistakable mark of age, though the date of construction is undetermined. Both are still private residences, with attractive grounds. From the continuity of the terraces, it is supposed that in other days only one spacious and beautiful terraced lawn was here. It is still beautiful with its carefully kept grassy sward, from which at irregular intervals, spring the majestic Norway maples, the black walnuts, the apple trees, and lilacs, the flowering almond, and other climbing and flowering shrubs, thick with picturesque bird homes, tenanted year after year by possibly the same line of robin, wren and oriole. In this magnetic atmosphere was born in 1781, the future governor of Georgia, John Forsythe. Can it be that some subtle and indefinable influence lurked in

IN KENMORE HALL.
The Remarkable Work About the Mantel and Ceilings Was Done by Hessian Prisoners, at Washington's Request

these magic surroundings, and left an ineffaceable impress for good upon the boy?

A delightful old colonial home is the brick structure on the east side of lower Main Street. It was built in 1764, and its present attractive appearance attests the quality of material in its construction, and also the discerning care with which the old home has ever been maintained. In Revolutionary times it was the residence of Dr. Charles Mortimer, the loved physician of Mary Washington. From the east window can be seen the graceful curves of the river, and the Stafford hills and dales still form a pretty picture in their verdant beauty and symmetry. Within the solid ivy covered brick wall encircling the premises two of the most magnificent trees of this section are noted, a Norway fir and a southern magnolia which, with other ornamental trees and shrubbery, and a charming rose garden, are such splendidly beautiful color schemes that one is constrained to linger in the presence of their beauty and age.

Across the street stands another solid brick residence, which, though of a later period in history, is equally beautiful. It is the one-time home of Matthew Fontaine Maury, one of America's greatest men. Its architecture, its interior decoration, its moss-covered, serpentine, brick walk leading to the old kitchen, and the fascinating flower garden, still radiant with old-time favorites, attest the age of this old home. Nowhere does the trumpet vine attain such luxuriant and graceful growth, and many other varieties of flowering shrubs and vines linger in the sun or throw their fragrance out on silent nights.

Two other landmarks in the list of charming homes built in bygone days — the latter part of the 18th century — each with enchanting grounds, are located one on Hanover, and one on upper Main Street. These are the old homes of Dr. James Carmichael, and Dr. Robert Welford. Lineal descendants occupy both of these premises today, and with the same loving care the bewildering tangles of beauty in leaf, bud, and blos-

*Betty Lewis — Mary Washington's daughter.

Federal, and Hazel, Hill

som, which characterize these alluring old garden spots, with their accompanying moss-grown brick walks, is continued. The Rappahannock river laves the east slope of the Welford garden. The picturesque windings of this river, and its wooded shores, together with glimpses of the ancient and interesting little village of Falmouth with "the decent Church that tops the neighboring hill," form a pleasing panorama. At the old Carmichael home, oak, walnut, apple, and mimosa trees, with a pretty arrangement of japonica, crepe myrtle, dogwood, lilac, English ivy, and other climbing and flowering shrubs, combine to make a setting of alluring beauty.

Nearby, and still on Hanover Street, is the old colonial residence known now as Federal Hill, the one time home of the distinguished attorney, Thomas Reade Rootes. Its white enamelled wainscoting, panelling, and other interior decorations; its colonial doorways, dormer windows, and spacious grounds where old-time favorites, both radiant and redolent are enclosed within its boxwood hedges and honeysuckle glen, all bear witness to a carefully preserved and graceful old age. Here too is the sun dial, its pedestal half concealed by luxuriant tangles.

Beautiful Hazel Hill, with its spreading grounds, the old-time residence of General John Minor; and the unusually attractive home on Princess Anne Street, the pre-revolution home of Charles Dick, supposed with every proof of accuracy to be the oldest house in town; Kenmore, with its storied frescoes, always associated with Betty Washington, sister of George, where graceful wood carving was done by Hessian prisoners, is magnificently beautiful; "the Sentry Box," on lower Main Street, the old home of General Hugh Mercer, though altered and modernized, has still the same attractive grounds, and because it was here that the country doctor, who was to be "General" Hugh Mercer and the tavern keeper who was to be "General" George Weedon gained the hearts and hands of pretty Isabella and Catherine Gordon, one infers that this was once the trysting place for many a gallant cava-

Beautiful Old "Chatham"

lier. All these historic spots deserve front rank in the realm of beautiful and interesting old age.

Among the pleasant places worthy of consideration, from an historic, and artistic viewpoint, none is more interesting than old Chatham, on Stafford Heights, directly across the Rappahannock from Fredericksburg. Situated on an eminence commanding an extended view up and down the picturesque river, and with glimpses of the church spires, and quaint roof tops of the old town, gleaming through the splendid shade trees dotting the grounds, it has stood for almost 200 years, a typical colonial Manor house, with characteristically beautiful proportions, an example of English material and English workmanship.

It was built in the year 1728 by that sterling patriot, William Fitzhugh. "Fitzhugh of Chatham," as he was known, was the descendant of the old Norman of the same name, progenitor of all of the race of Fitzhugh in Virginia. He was the intimate friend and classmate of William Pitt, Earl of Chatham, and the plans for the mansion on his large Virginia estate, which he named for the earl, are said, with every proof of accuracy, to have been drawn by Sir Christopher Wrenn.

Writers of long ago tell of the beautiful box-bordered garden at Chatham, and of the wonderful terraces, built by numberless slaves, "stepping down to the river like a giant's stairway." These latter still exist in their beauty, and form one of the chief attractions of the place, which has ever been famous, and whose most recent owner was the brilliant journalist, Mark Sullivan, and Mrs. Sullivan, who made their home there until recently.

William Fitzhugh, Esq., married Ann Bolling Randolph, and their daughter Mary, who married George Washington Parke Custis, of Arlington, was the mother of Mary Custis, the wife of General Robert E. Lee. A conversation between General Lee and Major J. Horace Lacy, (who with his family owned and occupied Chatham until the War Between the States) is illustrative of the devotion of both of these men for the old colonial homestead.

General Lee Spares Chatham

On the day before the battle of Fredericksburg, Major Lacy was at the headquarters battery of General Lee. By the aid of field glasses he saw across the river the white porches of his home filled with Federal officers, and simultaneously there was wafted on the breeze the strains of "Yankee Doodle" and "Hail Columbia." He requested General Lee to authorize the fire of the heavy guns, which would have laid Chatham in the dust. With a sad smile, General Lee refused to do so, and taking his seat on the trunk of an old tree, he said, "Major, I never permit the unnecessary effusion of blood. War is terrible enough at best to a Christian man; I hope yet to see you and your dear family happy in your old home. Do you know I love Chatham better than any place in the world except Arlington! I courted and won my dear wife under the shade of those trees."

Space does not permit a recital of the accomplishments of those who followed Mr. Fitzhugh, of Major Churchill Jones, of William Jones, his brother, or of Judge John Coalter.

The Lacys returned to Chatham after the war and occupied it until 1872.

The attractive interior with its hand-carved panels and corners is well worthy of detailed description, particularly the west bedchamber, with its alluring old fireplace and its high mantel, and is said to have been the room occupied by George and Martha Washington, who spent a day or two here during their honeymoon. Not alone have distinguished men of the Revolution reposed in this room, but John Randolph of Roanoke was also here, and later General Lee, and still later President Lincoln when he came to review the Union Army. Clara Barton, to whom suffering humanity owes such a debt of gratitude, was also here, a day or so previous to the battle of Fredericksburg, and Washington Irving and other notable men visited Major Lacy at the old mansion after the war.

The interesting and historic old estate, Fall Hill, which is now the attractive home of Mr. and Mrs. Fred H. Robinson, commands a view surpassing almost any near Fredericksburg. The house, built in 1738, is of the Georgian type of architec-

The Fall Hill Estate

ture, and its white panelling, its mantel pieces, and other decorations bear the impress of the care and taste with which the solid old brick structure was planned. In close proximity to the Falls Plantation, and the Falls of the Rappahannock river, this homestead well sustains its reputation as having had an artistic and romantic past, which is inseparably intertwined with the present.

Situated on a high eminence in Spotsylvania County, about two miles from Fredericksburg, it commands an entrancing view, for miles, of the glistening waters of the river, and the hills and dales of the Rappahannock Valley, with its smiling cornfields, and its cheerful apple orchards, and of the white pillared porches of Snowden, the charming seat adjacent.

It is a wonderful panorama. At the Falls are numberless moss-covered, age-old rocks, over which the waters flash and sparkle in the sunlight, fresh, soft, green, masses of grassy sward are here, dotted with the stately poplar, sycamore, and cedar trees; over there the gnarled old oak spreads its hoary branches, and honey locusts and elms are near, and climbing honeysuckle everywhere. Under the cedar tree, hollowed out of the flinty bosom of the big boulder, is Francis Thornton's punch-bowl, with "1720" and "F. T." engraved on the circle. All of this is close to the great house at Snowden.

Though not so old, the home of Mr. and Mrs. Frank C. Baldwin at "Snowden," has long passed the century mark, and the substantial brick structure, with its massive white pillared portico, its wealth of English ivy, wistaria, and other shrubs, its magnificent shade trees, planted irregularly on the extensive lawn, its flower garden on the west, in which peonies, hollyhocks, crepe myrtle, and other gay perennials vie with each other in glowing color and beauty, all unite to form a lovely spot. Nor can one forget that here General Lee and his staff, and citizens of Fredericksburg, sat in the old parlor twice before they decided that though the Federals carried out their threat to devastate Fredericksburg, they would not submit to an unjust demand, and for the only time in the war save at Appomatox and where Jackson died, tears gleamed in General Lee's eyes as he stepped in boots and gauntlets from "Snowden's" front porch to mount Traveler on the driveway.

The old Marye home, Brompton, on far-famed Marye's Heights, is today a handsome and imposing brick structure, with its white columned portico, and its impressive and enticing doorway, so suggestive of good cheer and hospitality. Each of these spots will appeal to all who see them, and each will bring back from the rich past a memory of its own. It is now the home of Capt. Maurice B. Rowe, who led Fredericksburg's Company K in the Spanish-American war.

Mannsfield Hall, a beautiful home below Fredericksburg, owned by the heirs of Capt. R. Conroy Vance is part of the original grant by the Virginia Company to Major Thomas Lawrence Smith in 1671, his duty under the grant being to keep at the mouth of the Massaponax a troop of 150 sharpshooters and to erect a fort as protection against Indians. For this he was granted land two miles north and two miles south of the Massaponax. Capt. and Mrs. Vance died tragically in the fearful Knickerbocker Theatre disaster in Washington in February, 1922.

The estate was known as Smithfield and the original house was of stone and two dwellings still standing are now being used. The present house built in 1805 was added to in 1906, and Smithfield was joined to Mannsfield, one of the Page family estates. Mann Page in 1749 built the beautiful old mansion of stone as a replica of the home of his second wife Judith Tayloe, of Mount Airy, in Richmond County. This house was burned at the close of the Civil War by accident, by the North Carolina soldiers returning home.

The Mannsfield Hall estate of today practically marks the right and left of the contending armies during the battle of Fredericksburg, being bounded on the south by the old Mine Road to Hamilton's Crossing which is on the property. It was at Mannsfield that the great Virginia jurist, Judge Brooke was born, the property being owned by that family until sold in 1805 to the Pratts.

THE SENTRY BOX
Below, Where Gen. Mercer Lived. Above, Mansfield Hall, a Splendid Old Home

Church and School

How They Grew in the New World; Pathways to the Light.

In the spring of 1877, during the rectorate of Reverend E. C. Murdaugh at St. George's Church, questions arose as to certain forms of the Episcopal ritual. Some of the members of the congregation approving Dr. Murdaugh's views, believed them to be in perfect accord with the doctrines of the church, but others felt that the introduction of these debated minor forms was an innovation and tended towards a High Church ritual. These discussions were followed by the resignation of Dr. Murdaugh, and his followers assembled in old Citizen's Hall on the 7th day of August, 1877, and steps were there taken to organize Trinity Church.

Reverend Dr. Murdaugh was promptly called to the rectorship of the new church, and Reverend Robert J. McBryde was called from the chaplaincy of the University of Virginia, to fill the vacancy at St. George's. With the kindly good fellowship, the tact, and the piety characteristic of his Scotch ancestry, "he lived in accord with men of all persuasions" both in the Mother Church and the youthful Trinity.

This congregation first worshiped in the unoccupied Methodist Church on Hanover Street, but on Christmas Day, 1881, they assembled in their own attractive edifice, which had just been completed on the corner of Hanover and Prince Edward Streets. Through the efforts of the Reverend J. Green Shackelford, (who succeeded Dr. Murdaugh,) and the congregation, the debt was finally paid, and on February 12, 1890, the church was consecrated by Rt. Reverend Francis M. Whittle.

One of the prominent characteristics of this congregation has ever been the energy and perseverance with which they grapple discouraging problems, and the unfailing and stubborn

The First Baptist Church

optimism of its women, out of which is born that success which almost invariably crowns their oftentimes unpromising efforts. Reverend John F. W. Feild, the present rector, is a young man of unusual attainments, and under his able leadership the church is a vigorous organization. A handsome parish house has been built.

The Baptist Church

Very little credence has been put in the old superstition that an inauspicious beginning implies the promise of a good ending, but the Baptist Church here is a conspicuous example of the truth of the old saying.

In 1768 three Baptist zealots were imprisoned here on two charges: "for preaching the gospel contrary to law," and, to use the words of the attorney bringing the second charge, "May it please your worships, these men cannot meet a man upon the road, but they must ram a text of scripture down his throat." But this intrepid trio continued to preach their doctrine, and to sing their hymns from the grated doors and windows of their prison cells, and each day drew crowds of awed and interested listeners.

To the Rev. Andrew Broaddus, who organized the Church here in 1804, to Reverend Thomas S. Dunaway, whose pastorate covered a period of thirty-two years, to Reverend Emerson L. Swift, the present efficient pastor, and many other able and faithful men, is the church indebted for the largest membership in church and Sunday School in the city, the communion roll numbering twelve hundred and eighty-nine members, and eight hundred and twenty-eight officers, teachers, and pupils of the Sunday School.

The present large and splendidly equipped building on the corner of Princess Anne and Amelia Streets was erected in 1854, under the pastorate of Reverend William F. Broaddus, and has had frequent additions as the increasing activities and congregations demanded. Dr. Broaddus conducted a successful school for young women in the basement of his church for several years preceding the War between the States.

The Presbyterian Church

To the Presbyterians belongs the distinction of having the oldest house of worship in the town. The present brick edifice on George Street was erected in 1833, the ground having been donated by Mrs. Robert Patton, the daughter of General Hugh Mercer. At the time of the coming of Reverend Samuel B. Wilson, as a domestic missionary in 1806, there were two Presbyterians in the town — surely an unpromising outlook.

This was about the time of the critical period in the life of the Episcopal Church in Virginia. For various reasons many of St. George's congregation had become dissatisfied. This fact strengthened by the forceful intellectuality, and the magnetic sympathy of Dr. Wilson, brought about the subsequent rapid growth of Presbyterianism, and proved that the psychological moment had arrived for its development here. In 1810 their first house of worship was built on the corner of Amelia and Charles Streets.

Adjacent to the present church on Princess Ann Street is the beautiful chapel, built of Spotsylvania granite, through the donation of the late Mr. Seth B. French of New York, in memory of a much loved daughter.

Dr. Wilson resigned his pastorate in 1841, and among the names of his efficient successors are Rev. A. A. Hodge, D. D., Rev. Thomas Walker Gilmer, Rev. James Power Smith, and the present much loved pastor, Rev. Robert C. Gilmore.

Dr. Wilson organized the female school which was taught for years by him at his residence on Charles and Lewis Streets, the former home of Mary Ball Washington. One of his teachers, Miss Mary Ralls, continued this school with great success, and admitted boys. How interesting would be the register of this old school, if it were available today! The older residents of the town remember well, and with pleasure, some of the men who were educated there, and won distinction in their chosen fields. Among others are Judge William

The Methodist Church

S. Barton, John A. Elder, Judge Peter Gray, of Texas, Dr. Howard Barton, of Lexington, Dr. Robert Welford, Lieutenant-Governor John L. Marye, Byrd Stevenson, attorney, and the Virginian historian, Robert R. Howison, LL. D.

Dr. Francis A. March, the renowned philologist, and for years president of Lafayette College, taught school here for several years, assisting Reverend George W. McPhail, the Presbyterian minister who succeeded Dr. Wilson. Dr. March married Miss Mildred Conway, one of his pupils, and General Peyton Conway March, so well known in military circles, is a son of his, and is claimed by Fredericksburg, though he was not born here.

The Methodist Church

Shortly after the Revolution, the Methodists began to hold services here. It is thought that for some years they had their meetings at private residences, as there is no record of a house of worship until 1822, when a church was erected on George Street, in the rear of where Hurkamp Park now is. Reverend "Father" Kobler began his ministry here in 1789, and continued for more than half a century. He died in 1843, and his ashes, with those of his wife, repose today beneath the pulpit of the present church. As a result of his godliness and assiduity, combined with the fervor and zeal characteristic of that communion, the Methodists, under the leadership of faithful men, have enjoyed a successive series of prosperous years, materially and spiritually, culminating today in a handsome, modern brick edifice on Hanover Street, well equipped for its many activities, and a large membership both in Church and Sunday School. Reverend H. L. Hout, the present pastor, is a conscientious, capable, and intelligent leader.

Roman Catholic

Until a sermon of unusual ability and power was delivered here in 1856, by Bishop McGill, of the Roman Catholic faith, that denomination had no organization of any kind. This event, together with the energy and enthusiasm of the small band of disciples of that faith, was the impetus which forwarded the establishment of the church here in 1859. The visits of Bishop Gibbons — the late Cardinal — and Bishop Keene greatly strengthened the prospects of the church, and though its membership roll is not a long one, it embraces today some of our solid and successful citizens. They have erected a neat brick church, and comfortable parsonage adjacent on Princess Anne Street. The priests who have officiated have been men deserving the high esteem of the community, and well able to carry on; the genial Father Thomas B. Martin is the present priest in charge.

The Campbellite Church

An inconspicuous red brick building on Main Street which has the undeniable stamp of age, though decorated with a new and modern front, is the Christian, or Campbellite Church, built in 1834. This was only two years after Alexander Campbell, the eloquent founder of the sect, came here to expound his creed, and to organize his church. Its little band of workers has passed through many stages of discouragement, but with fortitude and energy they have again and again revivified the spark of life, which at times seemed to burn so low. The building was used, during the War between the States, as a hospital. Under the leadership of Reverend Landon Cutler, Reverend Cephas Shelburne, Reverend Samuel H. Forrer, and others, with the labors of the present pastor, Reverend Daniel E. Motley, the membership has of late been greatly increased. The Bible used by Alexander Campbell on some of his visits here, is a highly esteemed relic.

Some Schools of Fredericksburg

The Public School system was established here as early as 1870. At first the schools were not well patronized, owing in part to the unusual and well-merited success of the private schools, and old-time prejudice against new methods, then termed "socialistic." Their popularity increased with their efficiency, prejudice was entirely eliminated, and to-day we

The State Normal School

have a splendid brick building on Main and Lewis Streets, which houses the elementary grades, well-equipped and with a commodious auditorium.

The handsome high school building on Liberty street has been completed within the past year. It cost 125,000 and is a credit to the town. The chief problem here is the lack of room to accommodate the unexpectedly increasing number of lads and lasses who present themselves on the opening September morn. More than several times have the efficient and painstaking principal and teachers congratulated themselves on acquiring adequate conditions for placing the pupils, when in an incredibly short time, "congestion," and "half-day sessions," are again topics in school circles.

The State Normal

The crowning glory of Fredericksburg in the educational line and probably the most far-reaching in its benefits and results is the State Normal School, established here by Act of the Virginia legislature in 1908, State Senator C. O'Conor Goolrick being most active in securing its location here. The massive buildings crown the apex of one of the most picturesque slopes on the left of the far-famed Marye's Heights. An institution of this caliber, in order to radiate the best in every line of its many activities, must be apart from the business, social, and commercial life of the community, and yet near enough to benefit from the many obvious advantages its proximity to such a center affords. Ahe Normal School fully meets this condition. The drive of about a mile from the center of the town is an interesting one, and, when the summit of the hill is reached, the driveway circles around the imposing brick structures; the Administration Building, Frances Willard Hall, Virginia Hall, Monroe Hall, and others. To the east, in all its historic pride lies the ancient city. To the west, beyond the carefully kept, and attractive campus, and over the Athletic Field, nothing is visible but fields and forests and rolling hills,—nature's handiwork,—and, as the eye sweeps

NEAR BLOODY ANGLE
Above: Monument Where General Sedgwick Was Killed by a Confederate Sharpshooter. Below: Battle Scarred Salem Church.

the horizon, it is arrested by more hills and dales of that region of our state named in honor of that daring and picturesque character, "The Knight of the Golden Horseshoe."

Under President A. B. Chandler, Jr., and a faculty of teachers chosen to provide that type of instruction calculated to prepare young women for successful vocations, the school is a success.

SCHOOLS OF OLD

If justice were done to each of the excellent schools of varying characteristics, in the old days of Fredericksburg, many times the space allotted to this subject would be infringed upon. But at the risk of this infringement, the names of some of the local educators of other days must be included. Mr. Thomas H. Hanson was sometime Master of the Fredericksburg Academy, that old school which is said to have begun its existence on Gunnery Green, which in its early days disseminated the seeds of learning to many youths, who afterwards became distinguished statesman. Messrs. Powell and Morrison were principals of a girl's school in old Citizens Hall; Mr. John Goolrick and son George educated some of our most influential citizens of the past generation; Judge Richard H. Coleman taught a school for boys at Kenmore, and also at Hazel Hill; Mrs. John Peyton Little conducted a popular school for girls at her residence, the old Union House on Main Street; Colonel W. Winston Fontaine had a large school for girls, and at a later period Miss Frank Chinn, Miss Tillie Slaughter, and others, and still later Miss Willie Schooler (Mrs. Frank Page) conducted elementary schools, which by reason of their efficiency gained great popularity. The school of the late Charles Wisner was largely attended by both sexes.

FREDERICKSBURG COLLEGE

The interesting building (now the home of Mr. W. E. Lang, Smithsonia, has almost since its construction been closely associated with the religious or educational life of the

Colored Institutions

community. In it for years was conducted successfully, under various teachers, a school for young ladies, always under Presbyterian management. For years it housed some of the departments of the Presbyterian Home and School, of which that popular and efficient institution, familiarly known as The Fredericksburg College was a part.

Founded in 1893 by Reverend A. P. Saunders, D. D., the beneficial activities of this institution continued until 1915. Not only were the widows and orphans of Presbyterian ministers the beneficiaries in many ways, but it afforded unusually fine opportunities to the youth of the town, and surrounding country, not only in the usual college courses, but in its school of music and art as well. In many instances its graduates have distinguished themselves at the University of Virginia, Johns Hopkins, and elsewhere.

Colored Institutions

The colored citizens of the town — and the phrase is synonymous with law-abiding, respectful and inteligent citizens—have shown commendable energy and interest in their churches and schools, as is manifested in the substantial buildings housing their religious and educational activities. Three churches, all of the Baptist denomination, each with its own pastor, hold services regularly. Each has a large congregation and a flourishing Sunday School. Though the equipment of both high and graded schools is only fair, the corps of teachers, all of their own race, is as efficient as anywhere in the State.

"Shiloh Old Site" and "Shiloh New Site" are the leading colored churches, and each of these has been steadily growing for years.

The Church of England

First in Virginia, the Church of England Has the Longest History.

It has been said, and by reliable searchers after historical truths, that the first Christian shrine in America was built by Spanish missionaries, and on the site where now stands the City of Fredericksburg. But as no proof has been found, we relinquish this claim, and find our first authentic beginnings of Christianity in an old entry found in the records of Spotsylvania County, 1724: Information brought by Thomas Chew, Church warden, against John Diggs for absenting himself from the place of divine worship; he is fined ten shillings, or one hundred pounds of tobacco, or must receive corporal punishment in lieu thereof, as the law directs." These were days in the infant colony when religious freedom had no place. Legislation was paramount and, though never since those times has the need of the gospel been so obvious, the people had to accept the Minister that "His Honorable, the Governor," sent them.

St. George's parish and the early history of Fredericksburg are inseparably linked. Affairs of Church and affairs of State were embodied in one system.

In the main the character and manner of living of the early ministers of the Church of England here were not in accord with the dignity of their mission. Incidents so indicating were not at all unusual: on one occasion a clergyman of gigantic size and strength had a rough and tumble fight with members of his vestry, in which the laymen were knocked out. The burly Englishman took as his text the following Sunday, "And I contended with them, and cursed them, and smote certain of them, and plucked off their hair." Bishop Meade says, "Surely God must have greatly loved this branch of his Holy Catholic Church, or he would not have borne so long with her unfaithfulness, and so readily forgiven her sins."

Some of the Early Rectors

But happily, all those who in the olden days ministered in the Parish of St. George were not of this type.

St. George's Parish and the County of Spotsylvania were contemporaneously established in 1720. The first official record of the parish extant is the notice of the vestry meeting on January 16, 1726, at Mattaponi, one of the three churches then in the parish, Reverend Theodosius Staige, minister. Reverend Rodman Kennor succeeded Mr. Staige. It was not until the 10th of April, 1732, that Colonel Henry Willis contracted to build a church on the site of the present St. George's, seventy-five thousand pounds of tobacco being the consideration. After much discussion accompanied by usual excitement, the State urging its claims and the vestry not indifferent as to who "His Honorable, the Governor," would send them, the Reverend Patrick Henry, uncle of the famous Patrick Henry, became minister. Colonel Henry Willis and Colonel John Waller, "or he that first goes to Williamsburgh" is desired to return thanks to His Honor.

Reverend Patrick Henry resigned his charge in 1734, and Sir William Gooch, Governor, sent a Mr. Smith, who, on account of his "faithfulness or the contrary," was very generally disliked, and after two sermons, left. The names of two ministers, father and son, appear successively on the interesting old yellow rolls at this time, Reverend James Marye, Sr., and Reverend James Marye, Jr. who officiated at St. George's for almost half a century, and who were faithful and zealous. The salary of these men was fixed by law at sixteen thousand pounds of tobacco. It is impossible to compute with accuracy this equivalent in English money, "minister's tobacco" representing many varieties, and its value seeming to fluctuate. In general four pounds of tobacco equaled one shilling. The elder Marye married Letitia Mary Ann Staige, the sister of the first rector; and Yeamans Smith, who built the attractive country seat "Snowden" in 1806, married Ann Osborne, a daughter of James Marye, Jr. From these families are lineally descended many of the worshipers at old St. George's today.

The Oldest Cemetery Here

In 1751 the first bell, the gift of John Spotswood, was used. In 1755 the legislature passed an act directing that each parish should provide for the maintenance of the poor, thus the first "poor-house" was established. In 1722 an act was passed by the General Assembly relating to the churchyard, and authorizing the vestry to reduce the dimensions thereof. This small and interesting spot, so carefully maintained today, was used as "God's Acre," before the legal establishment of Fredericksburg in 1727. Contiguous to the church on the north, this little "City of the dead," is a grassy hillside, sloping gently to the east; and amid the sturdy elms and maples, the graceful fronds and purple blossoms of the wistaria and lilac, the old fashioned roses, the clinging ivy and periwinkle, rest the ashes of those who helped to make the Fredericksburg of long, long ago. We love to think of those noted personages sleeping there, that

> "It is not hard to be a part of the garden's pageantry
> When the heart climbs too, set free."

Colonel Fielding Lewis, of Kenmore, and his three infant grandchildren, sleep beneath the old stone steps of the church. William Paul, the brother of John Paul Jones, is under the linden tree. Archibald McPherson, the generous Scotchman and friend of the poor, sleeps under a tangle of ivy and roses. Reverend E. C. McGuire and his relict, Judith Lewis, great niece of General Washington lie close to the loved old church beneath the weeping willow. Under the shade of the same beautiful tree, sleeps the father of Martha Washington, Colonel John Dandridge of New Kent County. Others, well known, are not far away.

Reverend James Marye, Jr., a faithful scion of the Huguenot faith, taught a parochial school here, which George Washington as a youth attended. It is thought to have been at this school that he wrote, under Mr. Marye's dictation, his celebrated "Rules of Civility and Decent Behavior," the original of which is preserved among the country's archives. The

Washington's Last Attendance

faithful service of Reverend James Marye, Jr., ended with his death on October 1, 1780, and during seven years following the parish was without a minister.

In 1785 agreeably to the law passed in the legislature giving all Chrisitan denominations the privilege of incorporation, the people of St. George's Church met, and elected the following vestrymen: John Chew, John Steward, Mann Page, Thomas Colson, Thomas Crutcher, Daniel Branham, Thomas Sharp and James Lewis.

In 1787 Reverend Thomas Thornton was unanimously elected rector of the church. Steady faith, unaffected piety, ability to associate the dignity of the minister with the familiarity of the man, are some of the characteristics which his biographers have attributed to him, and which made him acceptable to all classes. It was during his ministrations that the Fredericksburg Academy was held in such high estimation. Many eminent men have attended this old school.

Four pews in the gallery of St. George's were reserved for the use of the professors and students. An interesting incident which occurred at this time is told by Judge John T. Lomax, then a small boy. An addition to the galleries had just been completed, when George Washington, with freshly won honors, came on what proved to be his last visit to his mother, and as usual attended service at St George's Church. Because of the presence of the hero, a great crowd gathered. Suddenly, during the service, there was heard from the galleries the sound of creaking timbers; this proved to be only the settling of the new rafters, which had not been well adjusted, but which caused great fear and excitement in the congregation.

After the resignation of Mr. Thornton in 1792, the following names appear on the church rolls, and follow each other in quick succession: Reverend John Woodville, James Stevenson, Abner Waugh, Samuel Low and George Strebeck. During the ministry of Reverend James Stevenson two institutions of learning were established, and the benefit and ad-

The Female Charity School

vantages derived therefrom are felt to this day. The male Charity School had its beginnings in 1795, with these gentlemen as subscribers: Benjamin Day, Charles Yates, Elisha Hall, William Lovell, Fontaine Maury, George French and Daniel Henderson.

Though this school ceased to exist years ago, there are still three stone tablets inset in the wall of the old building on Hanover Street, where the sessions of this school were held. (This building has been rejuvenated lately, and is now the home of the Christian Science Society.) These tablets are in memory of three of Fredericksburg's philanthropists, Archibald McPherson, who died in 1754, bequeathing his property to the poor of the town, Benjamin Day and Thomas Colson, whose services to the school were many and valuable and whose charity was broad.

The Female Charity School was established in 1802, by the women of St. George's parish, generously assisted financially by Miss Sophia Carter, of Prince William County, and is still maintained to this day; their present substantial brick building on upper Main Street has been occupied since 1836 and houses at the present time eight happy little maidens who, with their predecessors numbering into many hundreds, would probably, without its gracious influence have grown into womanhood without a spark of that light attained by education and religious influence.

But notwithstanding these blessings times grew sad for the Church of England in Virginia. The Revolution in which each was involved was destructive to the upbuilding of the Church and the growth of Virginia. The results of that war were many and far reaching. The church had been closely associated with that tyrannical government which the people had now thrown off. Its liturgy, its constitution, its ministry and members were naturally subjects of criticism, prejudice and abuse. Having had the strong right arm of a strong government for protection, it was now forced to stand alone, and it seemed for a while to totter, and almost to fall.

New Edifice Consecrated

Such were the conditions under which Reverend Edward C. McGuire took charge of St. George's Church in 1813. In writing of his reception here he says, "I was received with very little cordiality, in consequence I suppose of the shameful conduct of several ministers who preceded me in this place. . . . Under these disastrous circumstances, I commenced a career most unpromising in the estimation of men."

Nevertheless, this inexperienced young man of thirty years proved that by living himself the gospel of truth and love and preaching "simplicity and godly sincerity," he could overcome those difficulties implied in the hopeless condition which prevailed at the outset of his ministry, when, we are told, there were only eight or ten communicants of the church. But his long ministry of forty-five years was one of prosperity and blessing.

In 1816 the second church on the same site and this time a brick edifice, was consecrated and Bishop Moore confirmed a class of sixty persons. Reverend Philip Slaughter says in his history of St. George's Parish, published in 1847, "There is apparently but one thing wanting to the outward prosperity of this congregation and that is, room for its growth. . . . . . I trust that the parishioners will build such a house for God. . . . . as will be a fit monument for their thankfulness . . . . . a suitable reward to their venerable pastor for his life-long devotion to their service." His hope materialized, for in the fall of 1849 the present beautiful edifice was completed. A few years after the completion of this building, July 9, 1854, a fire occurred, and the church was damaged. The loss was covered by insurance, and the building quickly restored to its former beauty. There is an authenticated story told in connection with this fire; the day succeeding the fire there was found, on the Chatham bridge, the charred and blackened remnant of a leaf from an old Bible and almost the only words legible was the significant verse from Isaiah, *Our holy and our beautiful house, where our fathers praised Thee, is burned up with fire and all our pleasant things are laid waste.*

Some Notable Vestrymen

Shortly before the death of Dr. McGuire, in 1858, the climax of his ministry was realized in the class of eighty-eight souls, which he presented to Bishop Meade for confirmation. Reverend Alfred M. Randolph, afterwards beloved Bishop of the diocese, succeeded Dr. McGuire, and in chronological order came Rev. Magruder Maury, Rev. Edmund C. Murdaugh, D. D., Rev. Robert J. McBryde, Rev. J. K. Mason, Rev. William M. Clarke, Rev. William D. Smith, Rev. Robert J. McBryde, D. D., the second time, and Rev. John J. Lanier, scholar and author, who is the present rector.

These men were all more or less gifted with a high degree of mentality and spirituality. Of a later and another day they were potent agents in diffusing the blessed light which must emanate from the church.

For nearly two centuries St. George's Church, its three edifices each more costly and imposing than its predecessor, has commanded the summit of the hill at Princess Anne and George Streets. Its interesting tablets and beautiful windows tell in part, the story of its engaging past.

In glancing over that precious manuscript, the old parish vestry book, which numbers its birthdays by hundreds of years, names familiar to every student of American history are noted. Colonel Fielding Lewis is there and General Hugh Mercer, General George Weedon, and Colonel Charles Washington, also Dr. Charles Mortimer, the physician of Mary Washington. Others dear to the hearts of old Fredericksburgers are Reuben T. Thom, who held the unusual record of serving the vestry for a successive period of fifty-two years; Zachary Lewis, attorney to his majesty, the King of England; Lewis Willis, grandfather of Catherine, Princess Murat; Captain John Herndon, Francis Thornton, Ambrose Grayson, Francis Talliaferro, Robert Beverly; but for the fact that there is such a vast assemblage of names, interesting to the generation of today, an entertaining recital of them in this brief sketch, would be possible.

The 250th Birthday

Fredericksburg Celebrates an Anniversary

Many months were given to preparation for this greatest event in the modern history of Fredericksburg, the celebration of her 250th birthday as a chartered community. Much thought was spent on how best to portray the Town's history from the granting of the "Lease Lands" by Governor Berkley, in May, 1671, to be settled by the Colonists.

The entire city officially and individually had given itself up, practically, to staging a Celebration befitting the unique occasion. All the hard working committees declared things ready for the Morning of the 25th of May, when the ceremonies of the day would begin at nine o'clock with an official reception to delegates with credentials, and special guests of the city, at the Court House. Doubtful ones had not lacked prediction of failure, and they were confirmed in their fears when the early morning began with a thunder storm and downpour. The stout hearted and faithful who had carried on the work were, however, at their posts of duty, and gladly saw the sun break through just in time for the opening festivities. The entire city was elaborately decorated, flags flying and "the colors" displayed in bunting on every home and building. A program, replete with events, half solemn, gay or merry, was arranged for the day, of which every moment was taken up. Never before in its varied history did such an air of gayety envelop the city. Visitors flocked to Fredericksburg and long before the beginning thousands had gathered, sidewalks, steps and porches were crowded with merry throngs in carnival mood. While the thousands of visitors were pouring into the town by railroad and by highway the celebration was formally inaugurated when the official guests appeared at the courthouse and presented Chairman W. L. Brannan of the Celebration Committee, and Mayor J. Garnett King their credentials,

FEDERAL HILL.

Built by Judge Brooke, Brother of Surgeon Brooke, of the Bon Homme Richard

Real Indians In War Dance

which will become a part of the archives of the town. This formality took but a few minutes.

At nine thirty A. M., exercises were held on Lewis Street to mark the boundaries of the Lease Lands, which was done under the auspices of the A. P. V. A., one of whose members, Mrs. V. M. Fleming, had in searching old records, come across the forgotten document of the Lease Lands and worked hard for the celebration. A granite marker was unveiled with the following ceremonies: Mrs. D. D. Wheeler, President, presented the tablet in the name of the A. P. V. A.

Opening prayer — Rev. R. C. Gilmore.
Address — Dr. J. P. Smith, introduced by Dr. Barney.
Unveiling — by Jacquelin Smith, a descendant of Lawrence Smith, first Commander of the town.
Acceptance — Mayor J. Garnett King.
Benediction — Rev. J. J. Lanier.
These exercises were very impressive and largely attended.

Receptions, addresses by distinguished guests, parades of soldiers and marines, veterans of three wars and descendants of Indians were all on the program which followed and fascinated the crowds at various points. In front of the Princess Anne Hotel was presented a lively scene, with one of the bands of marines from Quantico playing on the balcony while throngs of gaily dressed women, citizens, officials and marine officers made up a remarkably brilliant ensemble.

One of the most interesting numbers of the morning program was an Indian War Dance, in costume, by members of the Rappahannock tribe of Indians, actual descendants of the men who concluded the first treaty with Capt. John Smith. This was in the City Park at 11:30 A. M. The tribal dances were most picturesque and were in keeping with the birthday celebration. A concert by the Marine Band followed the exhibition by the Indians. The other principal point of interest at the same time was Washington Avenue where the Fort Myer Cavalry Troop gave an exhibition of wonderful skill. These manoeuvers were magnificently executed and

The Distinguished Guests

received with enthusiastic applause by the crowd. The Troops fell in line at the whistle. The two platoons then broke from the center and executed column right and left respectively. The first platoon executed troopers by the left flank and the second platoon serpentined in and out. The whole troop spiraled and unwound at a gallop, then executed by fours by the left flank center and rode to the opposite end of the field.

A large platform at the north end of Washington Avenue held the speakers, and the specially invited guests. Among the distinguished guests and delegates present were His Excellency, Westmoreland Davis, his staff of 15 members, Mrs. Davis, Hon. Herbert L. Bridgman, member of the New York State Board of Regents and author, journalist and scientist, Hon. Chas. Beatty Alexander, vice-president general of the Society of the Cincinnati, and millionaire philanthropist, of New York, Gen. Smedley D. Butler, U. S. M. C., Quantico, Gen. John A. Lejeune, U. S. M. C., Senator Claude A. Swanson, Washington, Col. F. Nash Bilisoly, State Commissioner of Fisheries; Chief George Nelson, Rappahannock Indians; Chief G. N. Cooke, Pamunkies; Chief C. Costello, Mattaponi, Chief O. W. Adkins, Chickahominy, John Halsey, representing the Sons of Revolution of New Jersey; Mrs. Archibald R. Harmon, representative of the city of Philadelphia; Capt. M. W. Davis, commander of cavalry from Fort Myer; Major Walter Guest Kellog, Regent of the State of New York; Newbold Noyes, associate editor and part owner of the Washington Star; Major General Adelbert Cronkite, commander, 80th division U. S. Army and others. As a native of Fredericksburg a warm welcome was accorded to Admiral Robert S. Griffin, who has won fame and distinction in the U. S. Navy and he was accompanied by his son, Commander Griffin. Dr. Kate Waller Barrett, born in Stafford County, and a woman widely known for her activities in philanthropic and social work, was another who received marked attention.

Mayor J. Garnett King was the official host of the city, and so well were his arduous duties performed that no one felt neglected. The Chairman, President W. L. Brannan, of

Mr. C. B. Alexander's Address

the Chamber of Commerce, presided, and under his skillful direction these ceremonies were conducted harmoniously and impressively. Mr. Brannan did the hardest work in organizing the Anniversary Celebration and its success was largely due to his energies and efforts and efficiency.

Following the cavalry drill about 11:15 A. M., Hon. Chas. Beatty Alexander, LL. D., LITT. D., vice-president general of the Society of the Cincinnati and a Regent of the State of New York, was introduced by Judge John T. Goolrick and made the following address of which we quote a few words:

"When I was about ten years of age I was sent with my Aunt, Janett Alexander, the daughter of Archibald Alexander, of Rockbridge County, Virginia, to visit at Chatham, I can vividly recall the generous yet well-ordered life which prevailed at that time under the benign auspices of the beautiful Mrs. J. Horace Lacy, with her noble husband, and I remember the huge wood fires in every room and the delicious Virginia food. Each of us in the house, I remember, was furnished with a body servant who was charged with the duty of seeing that we were made thoroughly comfortable. I was shown the interesting tree under which it was said that General Washington and General Lee both proposed to their future wives and I am interested to learn that the Rev. James Power Smith, A. D. C. to Stonewall Jackson, also under that very tree proposed to the lovely Agnes Lacy, the daughter of the house."

In the afternoon, Hon. Herbert L. Bridgeman, of New York, delivered his address as orator of the day. He spoke vividly, holding his audience throughout his address, and dwelling upon appropriate topics that brought forth prolonged applause. The city considered itself fortunate in having so distinguished a man and such a brilliant speaker, as the leading orator.

Before Dr. Alexander completed his address, over in the City Park a few blocks away, real Rappahannock Indians,

Banquets and Luncheons

descendants of those redskins who inhabited this area, launched into a series of yells, with accompanying dances and waving of tomahawks over their heads, and gave to the people an exhibition of the tribal dance of their ancestors, a preliminary to an informal severance of diplomatic relations with pale faces or some other tribe of Indians that had incurred their enmity. This spectacular ceremony was accompanied by music from a band representing a modern fighting element, the marines.

Again the crowd scattered over the city. People kept open house that day. Besides the private entertaining, large dinners were served in Hurkamp Park, and other selected places to thousands of marines from Quantico, as well as to all those who came unprovided with their own luncheons. A banquet was given by the city at Princess Anne Hotel to two hundred invited guests. Prior to the luncheon a reception was held there by Governor Davis, who shook hands with hundreds of people. Practically a reception was in progress at this hotel during the whole morning. Many ladies had been appointed by the Chairman and the Mayor on the official Reception Committee. They met there at nine o'clock in the morning to greet the guests. The luncheon was beautifully appointed and served at round tables, holding eight. A long table extended across the end of the large dining hall, where sat Governor Davis and Mrs. Davis, the speakers and other distinguished guests, Mayor and Mrs. King, Chairman Brannan, Judge John T. Goolrick and other city officials and their wives. Music was furnished during the luncheon by the Franklin Orchestra of the city.

After the luncheon, the biggest event of the Celebration, the Parade started to move. It is not the part of this historian to describe the work or the executive ability of those in charge, that led up to the final accomplishment of this pageant of exquisite beauty, or the forty-five floats exhibited in this parade. The scenes were perfect and carried out the idea of the town's history. Mrs. L. L. Coghill, Chairman of this, the principal feature of the Anniversary Celebration, worked out the entire scheme giving her personal attention

The Order of Parade

to each float, in the outline of its general plan, details and coloring. The beauty and reality of the parade surprised even the most optimistic. The closest attention was paid to the genuine historical aspects of each period visualized, and the characters and costumes were wisely chosen. The parade was nearly two miles long, and took one hour to pass in review. A fleet of airplanes circled over the city and gave a modern touch to the picturesque setting.

To Mrs. Coghill and her committee the multitude paid tribute in applause.

Led by a platoon of police, the parade passed as follows: Chief Marshall Edgar M. Young and his two chief aides, W. S. Embrey and J. Conway Chichester. Three color-bearers, one each for the American flag, the Colonial flag and the Virginia State flag followed. The music for this, the first division, was furnished by the United States Cavalry Band from Fort Myer and behind it came Troop K, 3rd United States Cavalry, Fort Myer. The glistening brown horses and the snappy appearance of the troopers brought forth the plaudits of the crowds. The United States Marine Post Band, from Quantico, followed, heading the second division, which was composed entirely of floats giving Fredericksburg's 250 years in picture. This display arranged under the direction of Mrs. L. L. Coghill, brought forth most favorable comment. No important point in Fredericksburg's long series of historic events was overlooked.

It began with floats of the four tribes of Indians in this section which recognized the great king Powhatan as their ruler, the Mattaponi, Chickahominy, Pamunkey and the Rappahannock tribes. The war paint of the redskins stood out in deep contrast to the pure white of the floats. On down through the days of Capt. John Smith and the men who established a colony here came the floats, depicting and demonstrating in brilliant succession the history of the town in every aspect of its political and social life. There was Washington and his cherry tree, Washington as the student, John Paul Jones who once worked in a store here;

Some of The Beautiful Floats

Revolutionary generals; ducking stools, pillories and stocks; the peace ball attended by Washington and his officers; "To live and Die in Dixie," showing typical darkies before the war; "The Blue and Gray", Dr. James P. Smith, last of "Stonewall" Jackson's staff, who participated in other festivities during the day, and Maj. T. B. Robinson, of the Union Army, riding side by side in an old shay drawn by the principal motive power of that day, oxen. One of the purposes of the celebration of the city's 250th birthday was to acquaint the public with Fredericksburg's past, and certainly that past was visibly before the eyes of the onlookers. Each float in passing received its meed of praise and applause. It would be a pleasure to describe them all, but the scope of the present volume will permit only a brief sketch of this beautiful feature.

The Knights of the Golden Horseshoe, personified by the gallant boys of Spotsylvania, represented this splendid band of former Virginians whose ride across the mountains brought them everlasting fame

"Virginia" was truly regal in its setting. Between four white eagle topped columns a beautiful and stately young woman clad in white and gold draperies stood over the prostrate form of the tyrant imperiously proclaiming in her pose "Sic Semper Tyrannis", the proud motto of the State.

The shades of morning were used to make this one of the most attractive of the floats, it being our Dawn of Day. Pink draperies with morning glories twining over them—pink, blue, white and purple, presented a beautiful background for the figures of the typical group of men and women presenting and receiving the "Leased Land" commission from Governor Berkeley.

The float of the period of 1608, which well represented the story intended, was the Captain John Smith float. That distinguished man with his two companions, was shown mooring his boat, on the shore of the Rappahannock. An old Indian and his young son (real Indians of the Pamunkey tribe) were stepping into the boat, intensely interested in the beads and other baubles which Captain Smith temptingly holds out as barter.

An unique and most interesting feature was the coach containing "Col. Henry Willis" — the top man of the town — and Col. William Byrd and his fifteen year old wife going to visit at Willis Hill. The coach was mounted high and the body glass encased, with steps that let down; there were old time tallow candles in holders for light. Sitting in state with her lordly spouse and the top man of the town, was the quaint and pretty little fifteen year old bride, doubtless enjoying the mimic occasion as much as her predecessor did the real one.

The float "Revolutionary Generals of Fredericksburg" was one that brought much cheering. A group of popular young men in Colonial uniforms with swords and side arms, representing Washington, Mercer, Weedon and others, were the principals in this.

Following this came one representing our first postoffice. General Weedon, Postmaster; scene taken from the small room in the Rising Sun Tavern, and the characters all descendants of General Weedon.

The "Peace Ball" float was copied from the celebrated painting, a colored engraving of which (given by Mr. Gordon) hangs over the mantel in the Mary Washington House. This was gorgeous in decorations of black and gold, which threw into high relief the picturesque costumes and coloring of Colonial days. Mary Washington, her son George, and the young French lord Lafayette were the outstanding figures.

The Ducking Stool, showing also a Pillory, Stocks, and a refractory wife perched upon the stool about to receive a ducking, caused much hilarity.

The Battles of "Fredericksburg" and "Appomattox" were realistic in effect, the latter shown by an old Confederate soldier leaning on his musket with the beloved flag he followed for four years furled amidst the stacked guns.

Chorus Songs Are Thrilling

"To live and die in Dixie" may well be described as a scene typical of the "Old South." A negro cabin ornamented with pine saplings and an old darkey sitting at ease with his pipe, in the doorway, and just outside a contented "old Mammy," in characteristic pose. The really excellent pageant came down to the present day with 'Woman's Work." "The American Legion"—"Armistice" and "The Hope of the Future"—the latter an immense float filled with happy children Even after the passing of the last float there was little diminution of the masses of people on Washington Avenue—apparently their favorite stage setting

A Marine Band concert filled in an hour or more, delighting the audience with a wide range of selections.

Grouped on the immense platform a chorus of one hundred voices followed. The program was attractively arranged with a series of period songs, several of which were illustrated with tableaux. The solemn strains of "America" were thrillingly rendered amid patriotic scenes, the people standing between the monument to Mary the Mother of Washington, and that of the gallant Revolutionary General Hugh Mercer, and on ground consecrated by the blood of the armies of the North and the South in the Civil War where each army had planted, at different times, its guns, and on ground that belonged to Washington's family. The hills of the Rappahannock, once crowned so threateningly with battlements of artillery, echoed the volume of sound, until it rung across the valley.

"The Land of Sky Blue Water" a period song, rendered by Mr. Taylor Scott in his magnificent baritone, was illustrated with an Indian tableau posed by State Normal School students in costume. "Hail Columbia" by an entire chorus and "Drink to me only with Thine Eyes" a song of Colonial period, by male voices. "The Star Spangled Banner" period of 1812 was sung with tableau by American Soldiers.

Civil War Period: "Old Folks at Home," "The Roses Nowhere Bloom So Fair As In Virginia," tune of "Maryland,

"THE 250TH BIRTHDAY"
Three of the Floats in the Parade, May 21, 1921

My Maryland," "Carry Me Back to Ole Virginia," by a bevy of young girls attired in frocks of "the sixties."

The Battle Hymn of the Republic and Dixie with its ever inspiring melody were sung, and then the Spanish American War period exemplified by "A Hot Time in the Old Town To-Night."

The songs and tableaux of the World War period struck a more tender note, and revived in many hearts the anxieties and sorrows of that epoch in the World's History, when days of apprehension and sleepless nights were the "common fate of all." The Tableau shown with it, represented a Red Cross Nurse, a Soldier and a Sailor of the United States.

"Auld Lang Syne," sung by the Chorus, ended the Concert and the great crowd scattered like leaves before the wind, many hastening to attend private receptions, others to get ready for the public ball at the Princess Anne Hotel at which would gather all the notables who had helped to make the day successful. The Mayor of the City, Dr. King and Mrs. King, gave an official reception at their home on Prince Edward Street tendered to Governor and Mrs. Davis and other guests of the Anniversary occasion. Among the special guests present, in addition to Gov. and Mrs. Davis and staff, were Gen. and Mrs. John A. LeJeune and staff, Gen. Smedley D. Butler, Hon. Herbert L. Bridgman and Hon. Chas. B. Alexander. Several hundred citizens of the city called and met Fredericksburg's distinguished guests. The reception was a brilliant and most enjoyable affair.

Later Senator and Mrs. C. O'Conor Goolrick entertained at a smaller reception a number of their friends and some invited guests of the city, including many of those at the reception given by the Mayor.

The reception at "Kenmore" to all visiting men, and men citizens was one of the biggest affairs of the evening, and the hospitality of the host, Mr. H. A. Whitbeck, made the occasion especially pleasant. An hour or more was spent in good fellowship, the mingling of old friends and hearty greetings to new ones. "Kenmore," grand old mansion that it is, was resplendent under the lights and beautiful decorations and Mr. Whitbeck's party for the men was one of the most attractive of all the social events.

As a fitting climax to the unique celebration which will go down the annals of Fredericksburg as one of the greatest in its history, was a Colonial ball at Hotel Princess Anne. In the early part of the evening the hotel was crowded with a merry throng of guests which almost prohibited dancing for the lack of space. "The lobby, ladies' parlor and ball room were filled to overflowing with handsomely gowned women and men in evening clothes. With an unusually good orchestra from the Marine Post at Quantico supplying the music, the ball was opened by a grand march, led by Governor Westmoreland Davis and Mrs. Judge John T. Goolrick, who wore a handsome evening dress of sapphire blue."

As the evening advanced the crowd of spectators which occupied much of the floor space, thinned out and more room was available for the dancing couples. About midnight a supply of horns, confetti and streamers were distributed to all present and the dance assumed a merry cabaret aspect. The orchestra was full of pep, as were the dancers, and the scene was one of much gaiety and fun. Dancing continued until two o'clock Thursday morning, when lights were out and the gayest day in the long annals of the Picture City between the hills of the Rappahannock, "historic Fredericksburg," became one of her treasured memories; not to be forgotten, but to be kept alive with her traditions by the descendants of the splendid men and women who have made and preserved her history, and caused her to become known to the world.

Appendix

Thomas Jefferson in the Virginia Convention of 1776 was the successful patron and aggressive advocate of the resolution for the appointment of a Committee to revise certain laws in order that they might be in accordance with and conform to the changed status and conditions of the State, from a Colony of Great Britain to an independent sovereignty.

This Committee, consisting of Thomas Jefferson, George Mason of Gunston Hall, George Wythe, Edmund Pendleton and Thomas L. Lee, met in the Rising Sun Tavern in Fredericksburg on January 13, 1777, where they inaugurated and formulated bills of great and far reaching import, which were subsequently enacted into laws by the Legislature of Virginia and followed by the other thirteen Sates of the Confederation.

These four bills were then considered as forming a system by which every fibre of ancient or future aristocracy would be eradicated and a foundation laid for a government truly republican.

To only four of these we make reference—namely—

THE REPEAL OF THE OLD ENGLISH LAWS OF PRIMOGENITURE then the law of the State, by which the eldest son as a matter of law and right became by descent entitled to property rights and privileges above and beyond all other heirs:—

THE REPEAL OF ALL ENTAIL which would prevent the accumulation and perpetuation of wealth in select families and preserve the soil of the country for its people, thus promoting an equality of opportunity for the average citizen:—

THE ESTABLISHMENT OF PUBLIC EDUCATION AND OF ELEMENTARY SCHOOLS FOR ALL CHILDREN — OF COLLEGES TEACHING THE HIGHEST GRADE OF SCIENCE—From this has evolved the present public school system, and Jefferson being saturated with this idea commenced by the establishment of the University of Virginia. A great service performed by this Committee fostered and largely encouraged by Jefferson and Mason was its BILL FOR RELIGIOUS FREEDOM— which met with more active opposition than did the other three, for it did not become a law until 1785. By it the State received its charter of divorcement from the Church—religion and politics were separated. It provided "that henceforth no man could be compelled to frequent or support any religious worship place or ministry, but all men should be free to profess and by argument maintain their opinions in matters of religion and the same should in no wise diminish, enlarge or effect their civil capacity."

No elaborate or extended thesis or dissertation on the too apparent merits, virtue, value and importance of these measures, in this brief sketch, is attempted. The purpose really being, with emphasis, to declare without successful contradiction or any possible doubt or dispute *that in the Rising Sun Tavern at Fredericksburg on January* 13, 1777, these all pervading, all important laws of the greatest import were formulated and inaugurated by the Committee referred to.

INDEX

----, Adelina 160 B 43 44 Betty 166
  Billy 140 Charles 42 43 44
  Douglas 42 44 Judy 42 43 44
  Monk 99 Sally 43 William 76
ACKERMANN, Nick 13
ADAMS, 92 J Willard 145
  John Quincy 92
ADKINS, Chief O W 190
AFRICANUS, Scipio 151
AGASSIZ, 99
ALEXANDER, Archibald 191
  Chas B 197
  Chas Beatty 190 191
  Dr 191 Janett 191
ALLEN, 146 Miss 164
  Mrs 164 William 164
ALSOP, 163
AMBLER, Mary 137
AMES, Michael 38
ANDERSON, 62
  Gen 58
  John K 68
ARMISTEAD, Henry 145 148
ARMSTRONG, Maj 81
ARTHUR, Chester A 126 163
  Ellen Lewis 163
B, Mr 42 43
BAGNALL, Chirurgeon 15
  Dr 15 16
BAKER, 153
BALDWIN, F C 40
  Frank C 171
  Mrs 40 171
BALL, 130 131 Fanny 147 Joseph
  123 Mary 130 Mason 130
BANKHEAD, John 153
BARKSDALE, 58
BARNEY, Capt 118 Dr 189
  Joseph N 117
BARRETT, Kate Waller 190

BARTON, Clara 126 170 Gen 155
  Howard 176 Judge 155 Mary
  155 Thomas B 38 142 143
  William S 154 175 176
  William Stone 150
BAYARD, 77 Gen 51
BEALE, William C 143 Wm C 142
BEASLEY, Mrs 61
BEAUMARCHAIS, Count 137
BECK, William Henry 120
BENWICK, J B Jr 142
BERKELEY, Gov 194
BERKLEY, Gov 17 188
  William 14 17
BERNARD, 51
BERREY, John J 38
  Robert Banks 156
BERRY, 146
BESANT, Annie 100
BEVERLY, Henry 20 Robert 187
BILISOLY, F Nash 190
BLAND, 138
BOGGETH, William M 142
BONAPARTE, 139
BOWERING, A B 155
BRADDOCK, 79
BRADFORD, 146
BRADLEY, James H 38
BRANHAM, Daniel 184
BRANNAN, Chairman 192 Mr 191
  W L 188 190
BRAXTON, 42
  Carter 69 110
  Elliott M 163
  Elliott Muse 110 111
BRENT, 31 138 146
BRIDGEMAN, Herbert L 191
BRIDGMAN, Herbert L 190 197
BRIGGS, David 156
BRINTON, Christian 101

BROADDUS, Andrew 174 W F 38
    William F 174
BROOKE, Dr 146 Francis 144
    Judge 172 Laurens 78
    Robert 148
BROOKS, 146 Gen 62
BROWN, 146 Madam 100
BROWNING, 99
BRYAN, John Randolph 121
    Lt 121
BUCKNER, 18 John 17
    Mordecai 136 Thomas 14
BUFFINGTON, Mrs R B 163
BURNSIDE, 39 47 50 54 57 66 161
    Gen 38 42 48 49 52 53 55
    Maj Gen 39
BURROWS, Mr 132 Silas 132
BUTLER, Smedley D 190 197
BUTTERFIELD, Daniel 55 Gen
    159 Maj Gen 58
BYRD, 138 Col 20 21 Mrs 195
    William 195
CA'LINE, 43 46
CALHOUN, 92
CAMPBELL, Alexander 177
CARDWELL, John S 156
CARLYLE, 99 100
CARMICHAEL, 168 Dr 121 James
    167 Mrs Spotswood W 121
CARTER, 138 Betty 147 Charles
    135 Charles L 156 King 135
    Priscilla 137 Sophia 185
CARUTHERS, Mazie V 166
CARY, George 141
CATHERINE, Empress 85
    Princess Murat 187
CHAMBERLAIN, Mellin 94
CHANDLER, A B Jr 179
    Mr 61 105
CHARLES, Edward 79
CHATHAM, Earl of 169
CHEW, 146 John 184 John J 142
    145 John Jr 145 Robert S 68 145
    Thomas 181
CHICHESTER, J Conway 193

CHINN, Miss Frank 179
CHRISTIAN, Mr 137
CLARK, John Roger 110
CLARKE, 146 Benjamin 156 John
    Roger 110 Jonathan 110
    William 110 William M 187
CLEMENS, Mrs 100 Samuel 100
CLEVELAND, Grover 130
    President 131
COAKLEY, John 38
COALTER, Elizabeth 121
    John 121 170
COBB, 51 162 Gen 50 Senator 50
    T R R 51
COBBLEN, 100
COCKBURN, Adm 30
COGHILL, Mrs L L 192 193
COLBERT, 146
COLE, Charles 116
COLEMAN, Richard 150
    Richard H 179
COLSON, Thomas 184 185
COLSTON, 60
CONWAY, 100 Dana 100 Eustace
    150 Marguerite Daniel 98
    Mildred 176 Moncure 99 100
    Moncure Daniel 98 Mrs 100
    Peter V D 101 Walker Peyton 98
COOKE, Chief G N 190 Gen 50 J R
    50 James 38 John Esten 41
    John R 111
CORBIN, Farley 55
CORCORAN, Mr 103
CORNWALLIS, 81 82
COSTELLO, Chief C 190
COX, Abraham 38
CRITCHER, Col 38 John 150
CRONKITE, Adelbert 190
CROWDER, Jeremiah 20
CRUTCHER, Thomas 184
CRUTCHFIELD, 146 Edgar 68
CUMBERLAND, Duke of 79
CUSTIS, George Washington Parke
    169 Martha 71 137 Mary 52 169
    Nellie 73 Posey 137

CUTLER, Landon 177
CZAR, of Russia 96
D'ADHEMAR, Count 55
D'ESTAING, Count 93
D'ESTANG, Count 137
D'NOUVALLES, Count 137
DABNEY, R S 105
DALGREN, Capt 38
DANA, Ellen Davis 99
DANDRIDGE, John 183
DANIEL, Fred 103 John M 98 John W 131 Maria K 127 Peter 138 Peter V 157 R T 103 Senator 124
DARWIN, 100
DAVIS, Gov 192 197 Jefferson 56 103 158 John 134 M W 190 Mrs 190 192 197 Westmoreland 190 198
DAY, Benj 140 Benjamin 156 185
DECHARTRES, Duchess 77
DECRILLION, Duke 84
DEGRAFFENRIED, Baron 19
DEJUMONVILLE, M 71
DEMAURIER, 100
DEPARIS, Count 164
DICK, Charles 26 144 168
DICKENS, 100
DICKEY, Robert 143
DIGGS, John 181
DINWIDDIE, Gov 22 71
DOGGETT, Hugh S 68 157
DORNIN, Thomas 120
DOSWELL, 29 Temple 158
DUKE, of Cumberland 79
DUNAWAY, Thomas S 174
DUNMORE, 72 Lord 23 89 136
EARLY, Gen 58
EDGERLY, Surgeon 78
EDWARD VII, 163
ELDER, Jack 104 John A 102 176 Mr 103
ELIOT, George 100
ELSMERE, Robert 100
EMBREY, W S 193

EMBRY, Judge 145
EMERSON, 99 100
EMERY, J A 121
EMPEROR, of France 96
ENGLAND, Miss 121
ESSEX, Benj 149
EUSTACE, John 69 Lt 42 43 45
EVERETT, Edward 164
EWELL, 65
FAIRFAX, George William 72 Lord 71
FEATHERSTONE, Master 16
FEILD, John F W 174
FERNEYHOUGH, 146 John 147
FIELD, Cyrus 96
FITZHUGH, 137 138 Mary 169 Mr 170 Thomas 138 William 169
FLEMING, Mrs V M 131 V M 189
FONTAINE, W Winston 179
FORRER, Samuel H 177
FORSYTHE, John 51 149 160 166 Robert 149
FOUNTAINE, John 19
FRANKLIN, 48 49 51
FREDERICK, Prince of Wales 20
FRENCH, Dr 146 George 156 185 John 40 Seth B 175
FREUD, 100
G, Mr 42 43
GASKINS, Miss 98
GEORGE II, 20
GEORGE III, 20
GIBBONS, Bishop 177
GIBSON, 81 Capt 80
GILBERT, W S 100
GILL, Beverly T 38
GILLIS, Dr 146
GILMER, Thomas Walker 175
GILMORE, R C 189 Robert C 175
GLADSTONE, 89
GOOCH, William 182
GOODWIN, Thomas 156

GOOLRICK, 88
  C O'conor 178 197 Charles T 69
  Frances Bernard 41 George 179
  John 179 John T 41 145 191
  192 Mrs 129 Mrs C O'conor 197
  Mrs Frances B 127 Mrs Francis
  B 127 Mrs John T 198 Peter 69
  142 143 156 Robert Emmett 69
GORDON, 65 67 146 Bazil 20
  Catherine 168 Douglas H 40
  Isabella 80 168 Miss 135
  Mr 195
GOULDMAN, Henry R 157
GRANT, 39 66 67 68 Gen 64 67 68
  Lord 103
GRAY, 146 Peter 176
GRAYSON, Ambrose 187
GREGG, Gen 49 Maxey 49
GREGORY, 132 137 Miss 132
GRIFFIN, Commander 190
  Robert S 117 190
GUBB, E Bird 63
HALE, Miss 137
HALL, Dr 146 Elisha 185
HALSEY, John 190
HAMILTON, Col 68
HANCOCK, 67
HAND, Dr 146
HANSON, Thomas H 179
HARLAN, Judge 89
HARMON, Archibald R 190
HARRISON, 138
  Gunyon 69
  Samuel 40
HARVEY, William 156
HAWTHORNE, 99
HAYDEN, Jack 59
HAYES, President 162
HAYS, Gen 66 163
HAZARD, Josiah 157
HEDLER, Edmond 17
HEFLIN, George W 30
HENDERSON, Col 164
  Daniel 185
HENRY, 87 Patrick 21 25 136 182

HERNDON, 146 Ann 94 125
  Commander 116 Dabney M 125
  Dr 111 Ellen 126 Ellen Lewis
  125 163 James Carmichael 112
  John 187 John M 145 Miss 126
  W L 163 William Lewis 125
  Wm Lewis 115
HETH, 65
HETZEL, Margaret 129 Susan
  Riviere 129
HILL, 61 A P 59 60 104 Gen 105
HOBBIE, Master 70
HODGE, A A 175
HOLMES, Oliver Wendell 99
HOOE, Richardetta Mason 108
HOOKER, 39 48 49 55 58 59 60 61
  62 64 66 Gen 57 Joe 161 Maj
  Gen 54
HOUT, H L 176
HOWE, 17 Gen 81
HOWISON, Robert R 176
HUGHS, Arthur 100
HUMBOLDT, Alexander 94
HUMPHREYS, Gen 159
HUNT, Gaillard 89 Gillard 135
HUNTER, Edward 68
HUNTON, Eppa 157
HUXLEY, 100
INDIAN, Chief C Costello 190
  Chief G N Cooke 190 Chief
  George Nelson 190 Chief O W
  Adkins 190 King Powhatan 193
  Mosco 15
INGRAM, 146
IRVINE, 136 Brig Gen 137
IRVING, Washington 106 170
JACKSON, 48 49 58 59 60 103 161
  163 172 Andrew 130 132 153
  C F 50 51 Gen 55 61 105
  Mrs 61
  Stonewall 49 58 104 106 155
  157 164 191 194
JAMES, William 149
JARVIS, James 26
JAY, 84 John 83

JEFFERSON, 77 87 92 138 139 166 200 Joseph 100 Thomas 135 199
JENKINS, 146 A L 29 Gen 66 Wm 148
JOHNSON, 146 A L 69 Edward 67 Robert 136
JOHNSTON, 65 Joseph E 106 Richard 156
JONES, Betty Churchill 106 Burne 100 Churchill 170 John 76 John Paul 75 76 77 78 80 136 183 193 William 170 William Paul 75 76 136 183
JULIEN, John 26 144
KEENE, Bishop 177
KELLOG, Walter Guest 190
KENNOR, Rodman 182
KER, David C 156
KERSHAW, 50
KING, Dr 197 J Garnett 157 188 189 190 Mayor 192 Mrs 192 197
KING of Belgium, 96
KING of Denmark, 96
KING of England 187
KING of Portugal 96
KING of Spain 96
KIRKLAND, Dick 53
KNOW, Robert T 68
KNOX, James S 68 Robert S 69 Thomas F 38
KOBLER, Father 176
KOSCIUSCO, 85
LACY, 170 Agnes 191 Agnes Lucy 105 Horace J 169 J Horace 105 106 191 Maj 52 107 170 Mrs J Horace 191
LAFAYETTE, 24 71 77 84 90 93 141 Gen 27 75 139 140 141 Lord 195 Marquis De 137
LANG, W E 179
LANIER, J J 189 John J 187
LEAVELL, 163

LEE, 57 58 60 64 87 103 163 166 Alice 137 Betsy 137 Charles 135 Gen 40 43 45 47 48 51 52 54 55 56 58 59 61 62 65 67 68 155 162 163 170 171 191 Harry 135 Lucy Lightfoot 137 Ludwell 138 Richard Henry 138 Robert E 106 154 169 Thomas L 199 W H F 55
LEGG, John 26 148
LEIGH, Maj 60 61 105
LEJEUNE, John A 190 197 Mrs 197
LETEMEAIRE, Charles 77
LEVINSTON, Sukey 21
LEWIS, 137 138 141 146 Benjamin 83 84 Betty 90 93 135 146 147 167 Fielding 23 25 90 135 147 183 187 James 184 John 21 Judith 183 Merriweather 110 Robert 75 90 156 Zachary 187
LINCOLN, 161 Abe 100 President 158 162 170
LITTLE, Mrs John Peyton 179 William A 40
LITTLEPAGE, 85 87 Lewis 83 84 86
LIVINGSTONE, 100 Sukey 21
LOMAX, John T 184 John Tayloe 150
LONGFELLOW, 99 100
LONGSTREET, 65 Gen 66
LOVELL, William 185
LOW, Samuel 184
LOWE, T C S 58
LUCAS, Cornelius 152 Mary 140
LYNCH, Capt 119 M F 118
LYONS, Lord 163
MACKAY, Robert 156
MADISON, William 30
MAHOOD, Gen 82
MALLAM, Charles E 156
MARCH, Francis A 176 Mildred 176 Peyton Conway 176
MARSE, Ab 113 114

MARSHALL, 166 Anna Marie 110
  Chief Justice 25 110 137 John
  135 Mary 137 Thomas 25
MARTIN, Thomas B 177
MARYE, 29 172 Edward 69 James
  Jr 182 183 184 James Sr 182
  John 98 John L 142 143 176
  John L Jr 156 Letitia Mary Ann
  182
MASON, 87 166 200 Anne 137
  George 72 89 108 135 138 199 J
  K 187 John E 150 William Roy
  156
MAURICE, 100
MAURY, 94 110 146 Commander
  95 Commodore 125 Fontaine
  156 185 Magruder 187 Matthew
  Fontaine 93 96 119 125 167
  Richard L 119
MAXIMILIAN, 97
MAZZANNI, 100
MCBRYDE, Robert J 173 187
MCCLELLAN, 37
MCCLINTOCK, Professor 98
MCGILL, Bishop 176
MCGUIRE, Dr 187
  E C 183
  Edward C 186
  Hunter 61
  James 38
MCKENZIE, Alexander 76
MCLAW, 62
MCLAWS, Gen 58
MCPHAIL, George W 176
MCPHERSON, Archibald 28 97
  183 185
MCWILLIAMS, William 74 144
  156
MEADE, 66 Bishop 181 187
  Gen 64
MEAGHER, 50 Charles Francis 52
MEIGS, Postmaster General 31
MELCHERS, Gari 101
  Mr 102
  Mrs 102

MERCER, 30 80 82 83 138 141
  195 Brig Gen 81 Col 80 81 Gen
  82 88 136 140 Hugh 24 77 78
  79 83 87 135 136 168 175 187
  196 J 148 James 146 Peale 83
MIDDLETON, 146
MILL, 100
MINOR, 146 Commander 119
  Garret 156 George 118 John 26
  103 135 168 John Jr 148
MITCHELL, 53 John 52 John
  Purroy 53
MIXIMILIAN, 96
MONCURE, 138 R C L 98
MONROE, 178 James 24 31 91 135
  137 144
MOORE, Bishop 186 Thomas 164
MORRIS, 100
MORRISON, Lt 105 Mr 179
MORTIMER, Charles 26 92 144
  156 167 187 Dr 135 146
  Maria 92 137
MOTLEY, Daniel E 177 John 100
MOYLAN, 136 Stephen 137
MUNRO, Robert 79
MURAT, Princess 187
MURDAUGH, E C 173
  Edmund C 187
NAPOLEON, 50
NASSAU, 85 Prince 84 85
NEGRO, Frederick 147 George 146
  Little Bet 147 Old Bet 147 Scip
  151 Scipio 151 Scipio Africanus
  151 Tom 146
NELSON, Chief George 190
NEW, Castle Duke Of 163
NORTON, Wm H 38
NOYES, Newbold 190
NYE, William E 156
O'FERRALL, Gov 131
  T 131
O'REILY, John Boyle 52
OSBORNE, Ann 182
PAGE, Mann 131 172 184
  Mrs Frank 179

PATRICK, Gen 39 40 162
   Marsena R 37
PATTI, 160 Carlo 160
PATTON, Mrs Robert 175
   Sally 137
PAUL, William 75 76 136 183
PAYNE, 146
PEGRAM, 65 Gen 50
PELHAM, 48 49 162
PENDLETON, Edmund 199
PERRY, Adm 120
PETERKIN, 103
PHILLIPS, 55 John 141
PITT, William 169
POLK, President 108
POLLOCK, 152 John 69
POPE, Gen 37 The 96
PORTER, Ambassador 77
POSEY, Molly 137
POTEMPKIN, Prince 85
POWELL, Mr 179
PRATT, 172
PRINCE, of Wales 163
PROCTOR, Thomas F 68
PRYOR, Char's 44
QUINN, 110 Capt 16
RALEIGH, Sir Walter 138
RALLS, Mary 175
RANDOLPH, 138 Alfred M 187
   Ann Bolling 169 Edmund 136
   144 John 121 170 Maj 153 154
RANSOM, 50
REVERE, 143 Jas H 69
RHODES, 60
RICHARDS, John 26
ROBERTS, John H 38
ROBINSON, Fred H 170 John 20
   Mrs 170 T B 194
ROCHAMBEAU, 27 93
RODDY, Samuel 26
ROMERO, Ambassador 164
   Madam 164
ROOTES, Miss 51 Theo R 116
   Thomas R 51
   Thomas Reade 168

ROSE, Lawrence B 156
ROSSETTI, 100 Mrs 100
ROWE, A P 113 114 A W 29
   Absalom 157 Absalom P 113
   Alvin T 114 George H C 38
   J P 114 157 Josiah P 157
   M B 114
   Maurice B 69 172
   Mayor 114 130
ROYSTON, 18 John 14
   Thomas 17
RUDD, John 116
RUDDY, Samuel 144
RUGGLES, Daniel 37 68 108 158
   Daniel S 119
   Edward 119
   Gen 109
RYAN, Father 155
SARGENT, John Singer 101
SAUNDERS, A P 180
SAVAGE, Dr 125
   Susan Metcalf 124
SCHOOLER, Miss Willie 179
SCOTT, 58 116 Francis S 149 John
   140 156 John F 38 Taylor 196
   W D 119 William S 156
   Wm S 40
SEDGWICK, 57 59 62 65 161 163
   Gen 68 Maj Gen 58
SELDEN, 138
SEMPLE, Mayor 142 143 R B 143
   Robert B 142 Robert Baylor 156
SENER, James B 161 Joseph W
   157 161 Mrs 161
SEWARD, Wm H 162
SHACKELFORD, J Green 173
SHARP, Thomas 184
SHELBURNE, Cephas 177
SHEPHERD, 29 163 George 132
   Jack 21
SLAUGHTER, 146 Mayor 39 40
   Miss Tillie 179
   Montgomery 38 145 156
   Philip 186
   William 33 143

SMITH, 17 Augustine 20 Austin 19
　C Mason 120 Capt 15 17
　Captain 195 Dr 134 J P 189
　Jacquelin 189 James P 194
　James Power 60 61 104 130 175
　191 John 14 189 193 194
　Lawrence 17 18 144 189 Lt 61
　105 Maj 18 Mr 182 Thomas
　Lawrence 172 William D 187
　Yeamans 182
SMOCK, William 156
SOMERVILLE, James 144 156
SOMMERVILLE, John 26
SPOONER, 146
SPOTSWOOD, Gov 19
SPOTTSWOOD, 160 Alexander
　159 Gov 78 159 John 183
STAIGE, Letitia Mary Ann 182
　Theodosius 182
STANISLAUS, 85 86 Augustus
　King 85
STANLEY, 100
STANNARD, 29 John 141
STANSILAUS, 85
STAUNTON, Edward 162
STEVENS, Martha 51
STEVENSON, Byrd 176 James 184
STEWARD, John 184
STOKES, Sally 140
STONE, William S 156
STRACKOSH, Madam 160
STRAUS, 100
STREBECK, George 184
STUART, 48 49 61 162
　J E B 40 Jeb 55
SULLIVAN, 136 Mark 55 169
　Mrs 55 169
SUMNER, Gen 39
SWANSON, Claude A 190
SWIFT, Emerson L 174
SWINBURNE, 100
TALIAFERRO, 138
　Col 152 John 20
TALLIAFERRO, Francis 187
TANKARD, Mrs M F 128

TARLETON, 24 140
TAYLOE, 135 Judith 172
TAYLOR, 48 137 146 Murray 59
　William 156
TEMPLE, Benjamin 38
TENNYSON, 100 Alfred 99
THACKERAY, 73 163
THOM, Postmaster 122 Reuben 122
　Reuben T 187
THOMPSON, 146
THORBURN, Robert D 119
THOREAU, 99
THORNTON, Francis 171 187
　Mr 184 Thomas 184
TRAVERS, Raleigh 138
TRIPLETT, Mary 155
TURBERVILLE, 137
TWAIN, Mark 100
UPHAM, J H 112
VAN BUREN, 161
VANCE, Capt 172 Mrs 172 R
　Conroy 172
VIOMINEL, Baron 137
VONHUMBOLDT, 96
WAITE, Chief Justice 130 Mrs 130
WALES, Prince of 163
WALKER, 49 146 Edmund 152
　Joseph 148 156
WALLACE, 153 A Wellington 113
　145 C Wistar 111 H Lewis 157
　John H 156 Mrs John H 127
　Thomas P 157
WALLER, John 20 182
　Thomas W 69
WARD, Humphrey 100 Mrs 100
WARDE, Artemus 100
WARDEN, Henry 36
WARREN, 67 William 143
WASHINGTON, 24 40 50 72 75 79
　81 82 87 88 89 92 123 131 136
　137 139 146 164 166 193 194
　195 196 Augustine 70 Augustus
　71 Betty 24 135 146 168
　Bushrod 148 Charles 135 146
　187 Corbin 147

WASHINGTON (cont'd)
  Gen 23 24 27 124 140 183 191
  George 22 70 72 73 74 78 80 90
    93 132 135 139 146 147 148
    168 170 183 184 195 Hannah
    146 Jenny 137 John Augustine
    135 Lawrence 71 131 Martha
    170 183 Mary 72 89 93 124 128
    129 130 131 132 146 147 148
    153 166 167 187 195 196 Mary
    Ball 175 Mildred 132 Milly 147
    Mrs 27 71 72 123 140
    Samuel 135
WATSON, Elekiah 84
WAUGH, Abner 184
WAYNE, Anthony 136 140
WEEDON, 137 138 146
  Gen 136 140 195
  George 23 87 88 134 135 136
    156 168 187
  Mine Host 76 135
WEEMS, Parson 70
WELFORD, 168 Beverly R 143
  Charles 38 Robert 167 176
WELLFORD, Francis P 111
  Francis Preston 111 112
WHEELER, 146 D D 189
WHISTLER, 100 101
WHITBECK, H A 197
  Mr 198

WHITE, 146 Frances Seymour 126
  Mrs Frances Seymour 127 Mrs
  W Seymour 128 129 W Seymore
  157 W Seymour 128 131
  William H 142 143
WHITTLE, Francis M 173
WILCOX, 63 65 Gen 62
WILLARD, Frances 178
WILLIAMS, Charles 38 Jim 152
  Maj 38 William 26
WILLIS, Benj 24 E H 159 Henry 20
  21 182 195 Lewis 187 Marion
  24 Marion G 157 Mayor 24 Mrs
  159
WILLS, 115 Matthew Mcgrath 114
  Nat C 114
WILSON, Dr 176 Samuel 149
  Samuel B 175
WIRT, 136
WISNER, Charles 179
WOLESLEY, Lord 163
WOOD, Silas 143
WOODFORD, William 24 89
WOODVILLE, John 184
WRENN, Christopher 169 Lewis 38
WRIGHT, Thomas 141
WYTHE, George 199
YATES, 146 Charles 185
YOUNG, 146 Edgar M 193
ZEPPELIN, Count 55

www.ingramcontent.com/pod-product-compliance
Lightning Source LLC
Chambersburg PA
CBHW060116170426
43198CB00010B/919